Jessica Gale Friesen

This Will Not Break Me

Jessica Gale Friesen was born in St. Davids, Ontario, the oldest of three children. After obtaining her Bachelor of Science in Nursing from the University of Western Ontario, she practiced as a Registered Nurse in both acute and long-term care. After the birth of her second child, Jessica left health care and entered her family business in the petroleum industry – including petroleum delivery and a chain of gas stations and convenience stores.

Since joining the family business, Jessica has worked tirelessly, becoming the third-generation owner and Chief Executive Officer in 2014 of Gales Gas Bars. She has helped shape and advance the company's corporate and community presence and continues to explore ways to give back to the community. Jessica devotes her time serving on several boards and has achieved her Chartered Director designation.

Having suffered from postpartum depression after the birth of her first child, Jessica realized that her story may be able to help others. With that in mind, she has now put pen to paper with the publishing of her first book. Always looking for a new project or challenge, Jessica continues to write, run her company, sit on multiple boards, and play nurse to her two teens and husband.

Author: Jessica Gale Friesen
www.jessicagalefriesen.com

First Paperback Edition June 2021

PAPERBACK:	ISBN 978-1-7777562-0-8
EPUB:	ISBN 978-1-7777562-1-5
MOBI:	ISBN 978-1-7777562-2-2
KOBO:	ISBN 978-1-7777562-3-9
PDF:	ISBN 978-1-7777562-4-6

Published by Ownera Media
www.owneramedia.com

Ownera Media, a subsidiary of Ownera Group Inc., is committed to excellence in publishing and marketing industries. As established by the founders, *"the goal is to take your stories and connect them with others on a level you only once imagined."™"*

Published in Canada

This Will Not Break Me

Jessica Gale Friesen

 Ownera Media
A subsidiary of Ownera Group Inc. | Niagara Falls, Canada

For Ed, Eddie, and Camryn,

I'll always love you MORE.

A Note from the Author

It is important for the reader to understand that this book is my personal journey with postpartum depression and may not be indicative of what you or your loved one may be going through. However, if you or someone you know is struggling with being a new parent, I would strongly encourage you to seek out medical help.

There are many websites that offer guidance on postpartum depression, and they can be easily found. According to *The Free Dictionary*[1] the onset of postpartum depression can be gradual and may persist for many months. Mild to moderate cases are sometimes unrecognized by the women themselves, and they may feel ashamed if they are not coping and conceal their difficulties.

Feelings:
- Persistent low mood
- Inadequacy, failure, hopelessness, helplessness
- Exhaustion, emptiness, sadness, tearfulness
- Guilt, shame, worthlessness
- Confusion, anxiety, and panic
- Fear for the baby and of the baby
- Fear of being alone or going out

Behaviors:
- Lack of interest or pleasure in usual activities
- Insomnia or excessive sleep, nightmares
- Not eating or overeating
- Decreased energy and motivation
- Withdrawal from social contact
- Poor self-care
- Inability to cope with routine tasks

Thoughts:
- Inability to think clearly and make decisions
- Lack of concentration and poor memory
- Running away from everything
- Fear of being rejected by partner
- Worry about harm or death to partner or baby
- Ideas about suicide

There is no diagnostic test for postpartum depression.

Looking back on my journey, I can say that the only thing that never did occur — that would have made all the difference in the world — is for *one* person to really stop me and wholeheartedly ask *"How are you doing?"*. Not in the rhetorical sense, but in a true, deep, really honestly questioning way. You see, everyone knows it's hard when you have a baby. What those that have never experienced depression don't understand is that you can seemingly function perfectly normally, while spiralling internally. You can feel like you are being sucked into that black hole, toes stretched miles in front of you, pressure rising in your belly and chest, suffocating you — all while smiling and pretending that everything is just fine because you are *terrified* of someone finding out that you are not okay.

It's important to know that it is okay to not be okay. It's important to know that there are others that have experienced postpartum depression, and sometimes just having someone to talk to is the best medicine in the world. Someone to hold your head as you cry and admit that you are doubting your own decisions and skills. Someone to tell you that it's going to be okay. Someone to show you the silver linings that you sometimes can't see.

Sometimes, focusing on the silver linings is the only thing that will get you through the day. And it's important to always take things one day at a time.

As a society we need to continue in the fight to normalize the stigma surrounding mental health. We need to support those that are struggling, and empower them to advocate for themselves.

I hope this book starts a conversation about postpartum depression. I hope new or expectant moms read this and are able to reach out for help. I hope no one has to struggle like I did.

---

[1] *https://medical-dictionary.thefreedictionary.com/postpartum+depression*

INTRODUCTION

Imagine you are floating through space.

The space around you is dark — various degrees of black and dark gray. Far in the distance are points of gorgeous colours, in shades of green, purple, and blue. Farther out are brilliant points of bright spots that serve as a stark contrast to the dark — a rainbow of yellow, orange, red, and white. You see a comet, or a shooting star.

There are swirling galaxies in the distance. Occasionally, you see a cloud of interstellar dust. You are not afraid, as this is what you have always seen. It is silent, and the silence envelopes you like a blanket; comforting, soothing, and serene. It is what you have always known.

It's awesome. It's peaceful. It's perfect.

You continue to float... and you turn, as you give yourself different perspective of the beauty around you.

In the distance, you see a point of darkness — it's different from the rest; it's solid, total black. You are still not afraid, as it didn't appear to be something to be afraid of. As you stare, you are becoming curious about it... you continue to observe it, as it comes closer.

There is nothing there. Nothing to see. No shades, no points of light. Just nothing.

As it comes closer and closer, you are slowly becoming to feel alarmed... as if it's coming after you. You can hear something... a sort of strange, sucking noise — coming from this darkness.

Shoop, shoop, shoop.

You realize, "this must be it..." you have come upon your first black hole.

It quickly draws itself closer to you. So, you begin to feel your body is changing. It feels like your body is stretching or thinning out. You feel taut...you look at your skin, it's translucent as if others could see right through it. You can vaguely feel your toes; as if they are miles away from your head... and you look down to see them... somehow, they are farther down... and have taken on some unnatural forms. Then you notice, you can no longer feel your legs... they have been stretched... resembling thin and elongated life-sized toothpicks — it's bewildering... these unfamiliar legs couldn't possibly be yours... and it's just not possible that they are attached to you.

This huge black hole is pulling you even closer to itself. As you look down, your whole field of vision is now darkness. As you look up, you can still see the same brilliance you have always experienced, but this time, the shades and formation are somehow altered. It is as if the black hole has tainted everything you ever knew.

Your entire body continues to stretch, succumbing slowly into the black hole. Pressure is building in your belly and in your chest, strongly. It is becoming hard to breathe. Quick, shallow gulps of breaths are all you can manage. You look up, straining to see the stars, but they are farther and farther away. You look down, your toes are no longer visible. Your strength is depleting. The air is thinning as you hyper-ventilate. You feel a deep, intense throbbing extending from the bottom of your neck, and enveloping around your head, past your ears, until there are flashes of light in your eyes. You squeeze them tightly shut. Your eyes seem to be the only ones you can control.

Your arms are now stretching, and they are at your sides, lifeless. Useless. You suddenly realize that the black hole has taken complete control of your body, rendering you incapable of escape.

There is no one to help you. You are all alone. You have lost all control of your body. You feel a scream building in the pit of your stomach, rising past your heart, past your lungs, only to lodge in your throat — unable to escape!

Suddenly, for no understandable reason, the black hole loses its grip. You feel the pressure dissipate for a moment, but a moment is all you need. You are able to kick — fiercely, frantically. You are able to get your head and torso out.

Though that's as far as you'll get for now. Your legs are still stretched, your toes still appear miles away. You see the darkness lapping at your feet. You look up and see the brilliance of what your life has been.

You realize this isn't a dream. You realize this is your new reality.

The black hole will always be there. Just like you, the black hole was simply floating through space and time. It does not know the havoc it causes. How can it? It is an inanimate object. It knows not what it does.

Yet, it was set on its course hundreds of millions of years ago and it has spun through space ever since. Gobbling everything in its path. Its gravitational pull is the strongest in the universe, and if you come too close to it, you will fight for the rest of your life to not be devoured.

That is what anxiety feels like for me. That is what I see when I remember my postpartum depression. A black hole, always taunting. Threatening to take hold of me again if I lose control.

PROLOGUE

In North American society, there is a movement happening that aims to shed light on mental health. The ultimate goal, in my opinion, is to normalize the consideration of a person's mental health — that one day we will live in a society where struggling with depression, anxiety, or any other mental health syndrome, will be as widely accepted as the common cold, a broken arm, or cancer.

Having graduated with a Bachelor of Science in Nursing degree and practicing as a Registered Nurse before going into private business, health care is something extremely important to me. In my personal and professional opinion, there are three major roadblocks hindering the conversation.

One, mental health struggles are so *easily* hidden. A smile, a laugh, or the careful composition of one's face can convince others that a person is doing just fine. How can someone possibly be struggling if they are laughing? A recognizable example of this is the painful story of Robin Williams — he must have been a wonderful, happy, easy going individual since he presented as such and made so many people laugh. The truth is something far different. The truth is that the moments where we are with other people are few and far between in the grand course of a day. Even when we are surrounded by other people, it is so easy to feel so utterly *alone*. In a crowd of thousands, there may be not one other person looking at your face and actually *seeing* you.

Think of it, at a party, surrounded by friends, how many times do you really look at the faces of those that surround you when they don't know you are looking at them? How often do you take the time to stand on one side of a room and survey who is there, what they are doing, and what their body composure says about them? It is in the moments when you are not aware of others looking at you that allow you the opportunity to relax, and it is then that you may forget to keep that carefully composed mask on.

It is the times of solitude that are the hardest. It is in the early morning hours before venturing out of the house, or in the evenings after returning home. The times when you are in your home, where you should be the most relaxed, and are allowed the opportunity to let your guard down. The mask falls off, the laughter dies, and the smiles fade. This is when the need to 'perform' is no longer required. When the depression and anxiety that you have been fighting in public is able to creep in, and take over, until the next time you are in public. This is when your heart feels tight, your stomach is knotted, and you are just *so tired*. Tired of fighting, tired of putting up the pretense. This is when you are at your most vulnerable, and the weight of the world can feel like it is on your shoulders. This is when your thoughts can run away with you, and you can become so consumed by how you feel that measures are taken to do *whatever it takes* to make life easier. Alcoholism, drug abuse, suicidal ideation, self-harm, or, as in my case, a complete withdrawal from everyone and functioning only at the most absolutely necessary level for myself, my husband, and my son.

Second, no matter the best of intentions of others, most of them simply want to be able to bury their heads in the sand and not recognize that others may be struggling. Not that they don't want to help, they just don't know *how*. If they knew you were struggling, then they'd feel obligated to help, and their lives are easier if they do not acknowledge another person's hardships. If you actually acknowledged that you were struggling, that you weren't sure how to manage your life, or that you weren't sure if becoming a parent was as good of an idea as it had always seemed, where would that leave the other party? What would they do?

Again, think of it — someone asks you the rhetorical *"How are you?"* Too often we feel the proper reply is the obligatory *"I'm fine, how are you?"* But what if that didn't happen? What if the answer was *"Actually, I'm really having a tough day and I don't know what to do?"*

That would certainly get someone's attention!

Again, for most people the reply would be *"Oh, I'm so sorry to hear that, is there something I can do to help?"* Secretly, most of us would be thinking, *"Oh, jeez, I certainly don't know what to do. How do I get out of this conversation??"* Everyone in the world is struggling with something in their lives. We all have hardships and expect that those are private. A stiff upper lip, so to speak. We are dealing with our lives privately, why can't *you*?? Most people aren't aware of this inner monologue. They are simply aware that when told someone is struggling, they begin to be intimately aware of their own responses — palms sweating and heartbeat quickening. They were just trying to be polite. It was really a rhetorical question.

Things are changing. One of the positives of social media (of which there are very few, in my opinion) is that we can see the truth of other people — or at least the truth that they present. We can see that celebrities we admire are ordinary people that have mental health struggles just like us. Again, we are reminded of Robin Williams, but also hear directly from others such as Demi Lovato, Kristen Bell, Catherine Zeta-Jones, and Ryan Reynolds as they speak out about and advocate for mental health supports. These people have stepped up to not only state confidently that they have struggled with their mental health, but that they still struggle, and that they are succeeding, despite their struggles. They are advocating for mental health issues and shedding light on institutions that can support others.

Third, the realm of mental illness is so incredibly *vast*. Depression, anxiety, schizophrenia, bipolar disorder... and all the subcategories of each!

This is one of the reasons that I have written this book. Even today, with all the advocacy for mental health issues, there is still a stigma about postpartum depression. This has not changed in the fourteen years since my personal struggle. How can a parent possibly be anything but blissfully happy when they have a brand-new baby at home — one that they should love more than life itself? We, as a society, need to acknowledge that having a new baby is *not* all hearts and roses and rainbows. It is *HARD*. It is exhausting, both mentally and physically. The birth mother is experiencing hormone levels that she has never felt before, and her body is NOT her own — it is a tool to be used for the baby, from conception, nine months earlier. It takes a village to tend, as they used to say, but somehow, North American culture has shifted to one that expects parents to raise the child that they chose to have, with little to no assistance.

We need to start a conversation discussing postpartum depression specifically.

We need to acknowledge that it is hard being a new parent, and that it is OK to need help.

We need to watch for any signs that a new parent may be struggling; and we should be willing to advocate on their behalf. We need to support each other.

In the past, families were able to support themselves. Most families were large — five or more children was common. The older siblings would assist with raising the younger siblings, then when the older siblings had children of their own the younger siblings would assist with raising the new generation. In this way, by the time a person became a parent themselves, they would already have experience with babies — and would know what to expect, and how to manage.

These days, in North America, the typical family has two children — possibly three; this is considered to be a large family. I would argue that the incidence of postpartum depression has increased in the past hundred years, and that the size of today's families has a lot to do with this. With smaller families, there are people that have never even held a baby until they are a parent themselves. They have no prior experience with children. They have no idea how to manage when they have a baby.

Society has not kept up with the size of families though. The basic framework of support (larger families with each child learning how to care for babies through family ties) is no longer available, but it is still expected that parenting comes naturally, and that new parents *will figure things out*. A pat on the head, a confident smile from a friend, or that a family member is expected to be all the reassurance that is needed.

That was my reality.

I come from a family of three children, and I am the oldest. My brother is fifteen months younger than me, and my sister is not quite five years younger. I was far too small, when they were born, to gain any wisdom or experience as to raising a child. I never babysat children. Even my younger cousins, they were either born when I was very young, or lived so far away that I never experienced them as babies.

My husband, Ed, had two nieces and a nephew prior to our first child being born, but I certainly wasn't involved in the raising of them. I saw them from time to time but was not intimately involved in their childhood.

When I did venture down the road of truth and confess that I was overwhelmed with my new baby, I received the obligatory smile, pat on the head, and reassurance that I would *figure it out.* Not just once, but time and time again. This quickly caused me to stop divulging my struggles as I felt that I was not being heard.

In an ideal situation, every new parent would be able to seek guidance on every parenting question they had. But that is simply not realistic. New parents are sleep deprived, worried, and possibly even scared.

It is imperative for a relative, or someone that has a close enough relationship, to see the mother on a regular basis to monitor her, and advocate for her wellbeing if necessary. Whether that is the mother's partner, the mother's parent or sibling, her best friend, it does not matter — it could be anyone. It simply needs to be a person that cares deeply for the mother and her child. A person who wishes to educate themselves and learn how strangely postpartum depression can manifest, and a person strong enough to intervene, if necessary.

It is important to understand that postpartum depression can manifest in a variety of ways and that the support system for the new mother must have their eyes WIDE open in order to truly see what is happening. Literally, lives may be saved.

This book is about my personal journey with postpartum depression. By reading this book, you will see what my own experience with postpartum depression looked like. You will learn that postpartum depression manifests in many forms. It is the sum of those forms that indicate my own postpartum depression — any of my experiences could be considered insignificant in and of itself. But understand that what I share in this book, is intensely personal to me.

This book shows what my struggle was like, and hopefully opens the door to further conversations for new parents and their circle of support to have. I hope for this book to be a haven for a new mom — a safe place where you may find someone that understands what you are going through. Even if you never meet me, I hope you realize that you are not alone. And that you will see me as that one person who 'gets' it. A person who understands what you are feeling, even if you may be unable to put those co-relations into words. We all need our space, where we can feel like everything is going to be okay. Because *everything is going to be okay.*

This Will Not Break Me

CHAPTER 1

I walked into the banquet facility and my heart sunk. I immediately thought, *Oh, this is a LOT bigger than I was expecting it to be.* My palms became slick with sweat, and my heart rate elevated.

There were so many people that I couldn't see the table I was to be sitting at — but I knew it was going to be towards the front of the room, so I started heading in that direction.

It was a table of friends and colleagues, all of them there at my invitation. This was for two reasons. The first being that, as that year's lead sponsor of the capital campaign for our local branch of the United Way, I knew it was my duty to purchase a full-seat table as a sign of solidarity and further support of this charitable organization. The second being that, while my invitees knew that I was going to be speaking, there was not a soul in the room that knew exactly how personal I was going to be. My guests were a group of women from a variety of different areas of my life. I had met all of them through my business endeavours or my community involvement — and I looked to all of them as individuals I would go to for advice. Mentors, so to speak. Individuals that I looked up to, and I knew would provide the support I needed to address the crowd with the strength and vulnerability I needed to show.

I had been asked to speak in front of the crowd — explaining why I had made the decision to support the organization in such a large way, and hopefully to entice others to do the same.

I had purposely waited, until only a few minutes before the event began, to enter the room, despite being in the parking lot for twenty minutes just sitting and thinking. I don't typically get too nervous speaking in front of a crowd as it's something that I've done since I was a child. It's something that, while I wouldn't say I'm totally comfortable with, comes with the territory of being a business owner that is involved in her community. It is expected that I will speak from time to time, advocating for my business or for people or organizations that I am passionate about.

This time, though, was different. Suddenly, sitting in that parking lot, I was beginning to become extremely nervous. I watched as car after car pulled in. Local politicians, business owners, and young professionals, all exited their vehicles and walked to the front door. Friends and strangers alike. I hadn't realized how many people would be in attendance. It was too late to change my speech. There was no time. My throat went dry, my breathing became shallow and fast. I had written my speech days ago, and there had been multiple revisions as I wanted to ensure that my message was exactly right. I had practiced the speech, and exactly how I wanted to enunciate each word, multiple times. It had to be just right. Now, in my car, I am worried that I had gone too far — but there was no time to edit it. It was *'go time.'*

This was the United Way Campaign Kickoff Breakfast.

When I was asked to speak about why I committed to being the lead sponsor, I truly sat back and thought *'why?'* Why this organization? Why now?

The answer, when I got to the heart of it, was incredibly personal. Only those closest to me knew that I had suffered from postpartum depression after the birth of my first child. At the heart of a great many things that I do is the effort to ease others suffering, and to improve their quality of life — to a degree, this is directly caused by my own journey. United Way is an organization that helps in a great many capacities, with a goal to improve lives and build community. I was aligned with their mission, and very passionate about my community.

Once I realized that this was the crux of my *'why',* I felt I had to run with it — writing a speech that was heartfelt and totally honest, was very cathartic for me. It was going to be the first time I'll publicly state that I suffered from significant postpartum depression, and I know I'll bare my soul for the sake of an organization that could help others.

My life had changed considerably since becoming a mother. I am now a business owner, a professional, and a community leader. I am happy and confident. Though, this is a far cry from the 'me' that I had been after the birth of my first child. That 'me' had been the absolute opposite of the person I am now. I strongly felt that part of moving past, what I had experienced, meant admitting it publicly, and trying to help others that may be suffering in similar ways.

However, when I was writing my speech, I didn't realize that meant baring my soul to *five hundred* people from my own community.

Walking through the sea of people to my table, I saw dozens of faces of others that I knew, and even more dozens of faces of people that I didn't know. I sat at the table with my supporters and picked away at the breakfast placed in front of me. I couldn't eat more than a couple mouthfuls; and dared not drink the coffee as I was jittery enough already. My conversations were kept light, mostly about the sunny, clear September morning we were having. My stomach was doing flips as the master of ceremonies introduced the first speaker — the campaign chair, the colleague that had approached me about the sponsorship, hence the speech I was about to deliver.

I knew my turn was coming up. I opened my purse to pull out my written speech. I took one last sip of water, knowing that my dry throat would make it difficult to speak. For a moment, I wanted to run away and hide. For a moment, I was more terrified about this speech than anything else I had ever done in my career.

Instead, I took a deep breath and focused on why I had chosen to write the speech the way I did. I knew that I had written this speech with the right reasons in mind — to help my community. I took one more look around the room, and said, "*Well, there's no going back now.*" I could hear my mother's voice in my head saying, "*You'll be fine, Jessie Lea.*"

My name was being announced over the loud speakers, but it seemed to be muffled in my ears. I could hear my heart beating louder than any voices.

I rose from my seat, and slowly walked to the podium. I willed my hands to stop shaking, before looking out at the thousand eyes staring back at me. I took a deep breath… and from there, I began.

CHAPTER 2

The discovery that a woman is pregnant is a moment that is never forgotten. For some, this moment comes with fear, anxiety, and tears, for instance, in an unplanned pregnancy. For others, this is a moment that comes with an incredible amount of joy, relief, and a different kind of fear — the fear that the pregnancy might not lead to a healthy baby. There are thousands of other ways that this moment is also experienced, all along a continuum somewhere between the two.

The moment of first confirming my pregnancy was surreal. It was an intense moment of pride to have the opportunity to be a mother in the biological sense. It made me feel wholly female. I was so incredibly, wildly excited — my dreams were coming true.

The minutes leading up to this moment were tense. I had been anxiously waiting for Ed to leave, so I was alone at home, before pulling out the pregnancy test kit I kept stashed in my drawer of our bathroom.

I had purchased a pregnancy test a few months before — to be sure that I was ready when I needed it.

I felt shy when purchasing it. Somehow, despite being an adult with no reason to be ashamed, the purchase of the test was a public display of a choice I was making, and I was a very private person. Back then, there were no self-check out stations that I could use, and the staff at the local pharmacy were individuals that I saw time and again whenever I was there.

Ed and I had been married about four months earlier, and we wanted to start trying for a baby immediately. We were young. We both had good jobs, a house, and we wanted to be young parents. We both knew we have members, on both sides of our families, that had trouble having children of their own. But we didn't have details of that family history and weren't sure if that would mean we would have trouble as well. So, we wanted to start trying for a child as soon as we were married.

I had been tracking my monthly cycles since the wedding. Every time I had to start over at number one, I felt a bit of disappointment. I knew that these things took time, and that it may take a considerable amount of time since I had been on birth control for years. But I had never been a patient person.

Every month that went by, caused a little bit of sadness, for both me and Ed.

This time though, when I got to the twenty-eighth day, there was nothing to report. Day twenty-nine, day thirty.... by day thirty-five, I was beginning to think there might be something happening.

It was early October when we were at my parents' house for a traditional dinner the day before Canadian Thanksgiving. Thanksgiving and Christmas are the two most important holidays in my family. My mother always puts out an incredible spread, with turkey, ham, mashed potatoes, pumpkin pie.... all the good stuff. All homemade. It's still something I always look forward to. Family all in one room, enjoying food and each other's company.

After dinner, though, I thought perhaps for the first time, my mother had undercooked the turkey. I was feeling off. I discretely excused myself to have a few private moments where my queasy stomach and spinning head could calm down. I had been feeling a bit *'off'* for a few days — just odd things happening.

My hair seemed to be shedding at an increased rate. I was also experiencing vertigo at odd times and for no apparent reason. But the big signs were the nausea, and lack of a menstrual cycle.

Now, with no sign of my period in sight, I was going to have the opportunity to take the test! I was so excited I could barely sleep the night before. I stared at the ceiling, listening to my husband breathing. Knowing, deep in my soul, what the test would tell me the next morning. The directions said that the best time to take the test was first thing in the morning, and I was a person that always followed the directions.

As soon as I saw Ed in his car, driving down the road for work that morning, I went into our washroom. I then pulled out the test kit. The direction said, a careful aim and a watch were all that was required.

The aim was easy, but my patience to watch and wait, was more difficult.

"I would give it a minute more than required," I said to myself, *"just to be sure."*

I put the test stick carefully face down on my bathroom counter, set my watch to alarm for the allotted time frame, and I waited.

I paced back and forth in my bathroom, mumbling through different scenarios in my head…

"What else could cause the symptoms I was experiencing? A virus? A bit of bad turkey? But that won't explain the hair loss, though." as I snapped back to present.

I was hoping, with all my heart, that I was not incredibly mistaken. That I was correct in my diagnosis, and I wasn't going to be disappointed.

I had never wanted anything more in my life.

The alarm went off, in fact, it startled me as I'd been so wrapped up in my thoughts. I stared down at the pregnancy test stick, took a big breath, picked up the stick and looked.

"There were two lines at least," I was pretty sure, as I blinked, and talking to myself, *"there were two lines."*

I looked again, and there it was, one very visible, red line…

And as I looked closer, there was a second line… but it was very faint red, pinkish as it appeared — was I seeing things?

What the heck did that mean? *"What the heck did that mean?!"* I exclaimed.

Oh, the frustration! I sighed and fished the test kit packaging out of the garbage. The instructions were very clear:

No matter how faint the second line was, if a second line was present, it was a positive test.

WONDERFUL!

Already excited, *"just to be sure, though,"* I whispered, *"the test kit comes with a second stick."* So, I waited half an hour, then I aimed and waited for the second time.

This time, the second line was definite!

Two firm red lines.

My heart felt like it was exploding, and there were tears suddenly in my eyes...

In that moment, I became intensely *aware* of everything about my body. The way I was feeling, the nausea and vertigo, the few extra pounds that had appeared recently, and the way my clothes were fitting, just a bit differently. It was all for a reason.

I gave myself (and my baby) a hug, did a happy dance, and called my doctor.

I made an appointment for a few days later to have the bloodwork to absolutely confirm I was pregnant. Though, I didn't need the bloodwork to feel complete, I was absolutely confident and ecstatic about my pregnancy. Not only was I able to get pregnant, but it hadn't been the difficult task that Ed and I both feared.

Somehow, I knew, with absolute certainty, that there would be no problem carrying my baby to term. I was not scared. Something inside of me knew that there was nothing to fear. I was so sure of myself and *my baby.*

It was a sunny, warm October. That very day I drove to the nearest store for a greeting card. The store had limited selection, but I found the one that fit what I needed. I made the purchase and returned home. Then, I anxiously waited for Ed to arrive.

When he did, hours later, I was waiting for him on the front porch. I was becoming incredibly impatient. I remember him getting out of his car and walking up to the front porch. He smiled and gave me a kiss.

I had put the card on our bed, with the two positive test sticks, assuming that when Ed came home, he would first go to the bedroom to change out of his work clothes. And there he went!

By now, I was waiting in the living room. Oh, Ed's shout of joy is something I'll never forget...

He raced out of the bedroom fast, and into the living room where I was. He gave me a hug and bent down to hug my stomach as well.

It was a spectacular moment!

It was everything we had ever wanted.

Our dreams were coming true.

CHAPTER 3

For the most part, my pregnancy was mostly uneventful and rather textbook.

Ed and I spent countless nights debating names, or rather, debating girls' names. Ed and I had been together for eight years before marrying and the name of our son had been decided many years before I became pregnant. Our son was always going to be named Edward, after his dad, and we would call him Eddie. His middle name was a source of debate, but we finally settled on giving him two middle names — Robert and John, to honour both of our fathers.

Girls' names were proving to be more difficult. Ed didn't like any of the names that I liked. I loved the name Elizabeth — and dreamed of having a little Lizzy running around. *Lizzy*, a name I related to strength and a sense of adventure, rather than a *Beth*, which to me is the name of a quiet, shy, and reserved young girl. As a child, I had been quiet, shy, and reserved. I always wanted to ensure that my daughter was stronger than I had been as a child.

Ed was fine with Elizabeth — but as a middle name. He didn't like the name *Lizzy* or *Beth* and wanted to continue in the search for the name of our daughter. I must have thrown dozens at him — Stephanie, Stacey, Diana, and Carly. Carly was one that I really fought for. I like the hard "C", and again it was a name, like *Lizzy,* that evoked a picture in my mind of a girl that would be independent, strong, and wise.

At the time, the show *House* was fairly new, and we enjoyed watching it. One of the main characters was Dr. Allison Cameron — Dr. Cameron, or, as the other characters called her — just Cameron.

I was standing in our hallway on the way to our bedroom when I heard the name on the show. I stopped and turned around, just as Ed turned his head to look at me — both of us had the same thought at the same time.

And that is how we decided our daughter would be named Cameron Elizabeth. Or rather, in an effort to feminize the name slightly and be a little different with it, Camryn Elizabeth. Camryn — a name that was androgenous. A name that, if you heard it, you would not know she was a girl. You would not be able to judge her based on her name, and would not be able to assume she was weak just because she was female.

Already I was protecting my daughter from the sexism that I had experienced in society. She would be given every opportunity to succeed — starting with her name. In 2007, the world was a different place, and I was intimately aware of the stereotypical roles that were associated with a female versus a male. I would make sure my daughter had every opportunity to thrive. Camryn. She would be our Cammy.

So, we were going to have a little Edward Robert John or a little Camryn Elizabeth.

I loved the names. They were perfect. I didn't care if the baby was to be a boy or a girl, but my intuition told me it would be a girl. I was absolutely convinced. That is, until an ultrasound showed otherwise.

Ed and I had decided that we were not going to find out the sex of our baby. Early in my pregnancy, I had developed a cyst in my uterus — something to watch, but I'd been assured that it wasn't anything serious. The cyst itself quickly disappeared, but because of it, I had one or two extra ultrasounds that were not part of a routine pregnancy.

In February, I went for my third ultrasound, and soon after, I was at an appointment at my OB-GYN with Ed. Prior to that doctor's visit, I was sure I didn't want to know the sex of our baby. I had been of the opinion that this was one of the most special secrets that life had to offer. However, when the doctor asked if we wanted to know the sex of the baby, it was just too much for me. Knowing that the sex of my baby was printed on the piece of paper the doctor held in his hand, it was too tempting. At that moment, I just had to know what to call my baby, even though he or she wasn't due for another four months.

I looked at Ed. He laughed, knowing what I was thinking, and that he wouldn't win this argument.

We were having a boy. A boy!!

Ed was thrilled! *"Our baby would be the first grandson with the name Friesen — someone to carry on the family name,"* Ed said. I hadn't realized how important that was to him.

It didn't matter to me whether the baby was a boy or a girl. The most important thing, to both of us, was that the baby was healthy — and I was doing everything possible to ensure that would be the case.

My relationship with my son was growing every day — each day seemed to bring some kind of new experience. A kick from inside my belly, or an ultrasound picture, or something as exciting as buying pregnancy clothes for myself or something for my son. Each new experience made me more and more excited about becoming a mother, and I was slowly falling in love with my baby.

To me, I was a mother already. I had always been a planner — trying to anticipate every last detail so there were never any surprises. I read dozens of books about parenting, and asked friends and colleagues about their parenting experiences — saving tidbits of information in my mind to reflect upon later.

However, no matter how much I planned, there was no way to foresee the challenges the future would bring me.

Before becoming a mother, I was the perfect example of a 'Type A' personality. A perfectionist, ultra-competitive (though, unfortunately, not athletic), always in a rush, usually wound too tight. Through university I held a full-time academic schedule, worked part time during school and two jobs through the summer. I thought of it as a badge of honour, to be as busy as I was, a source of pride. I had little interest in a typical social life — the club scene wasn't for me, sleeping around wasn't for me, and doing drugs never interested me. I was hell-bent on making enough money for a down payment on a house, ensuring that I had savings in the bank.

I led a privileged childhood. I didn't know it at the time. In the tiny hamlet of St. Davids, Ontario, Canada, on what's known as 'The Bench' in Niagara on the Lake, I was the same as all the other kids around me. I was not special. If anything, I was a bit of an outcast. I wore K-Mart clothes, my parents drove a station wagon, my teeth were crooked, and I was far too skinny to even be called slim. I never had my own phone line, or my own television in my bedroom. Not like many of the other kids my age — almost all of us from affluent families.

By the time I graduated high school, I was extraordinarily aware that my parents were very well-off, and I was scared that my view of reality was so skewed that I didn't have a real grasp on how much money was needed to be financially independent. I was scared that I was unprepared for the real world. Until I felt financially secure, I was making what I felt were the 'right' decisions to set myself up to be the best mother I could be, ensuring that my kids would always have everything they needed. I had a goal, and that goal had a firm number, and I succeeded.

There is only so long that a person can run on that type of adrenaline though, and every now and then, I would crash. I was very sensitive, a harsh word from a friend would cause me to cry and deliberate for days, over what I did wrong, and what to do next. It would become my modus operandi in times of extreme stress — overthinking and worrying.

CHAPTER 4

As the months of my pregnancy went on, I was trying to plan for everything our baby could possibly need. Ed and I were enjoying preparing
for Eddie's arrival. Just in case the ultrasound was wrong the nursery was
painted a soft green that complimented the muted yellow curtains that had
been hanging when we purchased the house. I found a set of crib sheets in
a Winnie-the-Pooh pattern, which became the theme for the nursery. One
of my mother's friends was a gifted artist, and we were given two beautiful
Winnie-the-Pooh water colours on canvas she created to decorate the room.

I spent countless hours at Toys R Us, Sears, and Walmart looking at baby
stuff. *What kind of gadgets would we need? How many sleepers? Which brand
of diaper would be best?* All these questions going through my head.

There was such a huge selection of stuff, with seemingly no real rhyme or
reason. I was happily, blindly, insanely, in love with my baby. I was excited to
be in the stores planning for *my baby.*

Part of my preparation was research and education — I needed to learn
how to be a mother! I had never taken classes, this wasn't something they
taught us in high school, and my siblings and I were pretty close in age. I
hadn't really had any experience with babies yet, so I knew I'd need all the
help I could get!

What were the experts recommending as the 'right' ways of raising a child?
I had always been able to find the answers to my questions by asking those
around me for advice. How do you get a baby to sleep through the night?
What if the baby gets a diaper rash? What if the baby has colic? But a pat
on the head and *"you'll figure it out"* were the common responses, and that
simply did not help me. I needed to be ready for what my child would need
— and I poured over countless books to ensure I had the answers. I studied,
as if there would be an exam at the end of my pregnancy.

While the preparation was something I enjoyed, pregnancy was not without its challenges.

The first fourteen weeks of my pregnancy I suffered from significant morning sickness — which certainly should *not* be called morning sickness since it can come on at any time of the day or night. I experienced severe nausea that prevented me from wanting to eat most of the time, and the rare time that the nausea would subside, I would be so completely famished that I would eat whatever was the closest, as fast as I could — which would again cause the nausea. It was a wicked circle.

Once I was halfway through the second trimester though, the nausea let up permanently, and I was able to eat better. At Christmas time, when I would have been about three months along, I became sick with the flu. I had severe vomiting that caused dehydration. It was so severe that one evening I weighed myself, to check on the baby, in the only way I knew how, and I was alarmed to see I had lost ten pounds in only three days. I panicked — what if the baby was being affected by my illness?

We rushed to the local hospital's Emergency Room where I went through a series of tests and was assured I was simply suffering from a flu virus. I was severely dehydrated, but the baby would protect itself and take from me what it needed. However, the doctor did want to keep me in the Emergency Room for one night just to get some liquids back in me via intravenous. I spent Christmas day laying on the couch recovering.

The sickness I felt at Christmas was quickly forgotten though on New Years Day. It was a new year, and the year my son would be born. I was marking each day and what new experiences I noticed. The growth of my belly, the flutters that I was feeling that could have been gas, but may have been the baby moving. I was journaling the experience, and had registered on a website that would give me weekly updates as to what stage my baby would be at that week — the size of a pea, a grape, a nectarine, etc. The baby would have a spine, fingers, toes, and would be waving his arms and legs around in his spacious home. A home that was quickly becoming smaller.

New Years' Day was the first time I was absolutely sure I felt the baby move. A quick flutter, but one that was definitely more than just breakfast working its way through my digestive system. Another flutter, in the same spot, and a third. I put my hand on the spot and — again!! It was an incredible feeling. Knowing that my baby was growing, stretching, getting stronger every day. I was so excited to meet him. I was so excited to hold him. It was something that was incredibly intimate — just between Eddie and I. He wasn't moving enough that anyone else could feel him, though Ed tried valiantly to feel his son.

For another month or two, Eddie was mine and mine alone. He and I were a pair — already supporting each other and figuring everything out as we went, as everyone had told me we would. I had never had trouble figuring out how to manage in my life before and was confident that I was navigating my pregnancy in the best way possible.

Of course, as he continued to grow and his home continued to shrink, Ed was able to feel him. Eddie loved to wedge his foot up under my rib cage and it got to the point where I would have to massage it back down. It was always on the right side, and to this day I can still remember the feeling.

As the months went on, it became a bit of a game — I would poke my belly and my baby would kick me back! It was an incredible experience that is hard to put into words. I was soon able to see his foot pushing against the wall of my uterus. It was amazingly surreal — I felt that I was already a mother, even though I hadn't given birth yet. Somehow, being able to see and feel him, made everything much more real as if I'd been playing pretend before that.

As Eddie grew, he became a bit of an acrobat in my belly — doing flips and spins. One morning I was all alone, enjoying a lazy sleep in, and just laying in bed, when my whole belly did one big barrel roll. It was an odd, unsettling feeling — and I had to have my first chat with my son saying that was a bit much. I began talking to my belly, and developing a relationship with my son, while he was still in the womb.

Before conception, I had been taking measures to ensure the best health and development for my baby — trying to put myself on the right path, even before I knew I was pregnant. Things such as taking Folic Acid, not drinking alcohol, and staying away from deli meats and soft cheeses, all for my future baby. Once I knew I was pregnant, those things all continued, but I also started researching ways that I could bond with my baby and further promote an excellent start to his life. I had read that playing classical music would soothe the baby and stimulate brain development. I bought a set of headphones and put them on my belly — playing Mozart, Beethoven, and Tchaikovsky. While I can't say he enjoyed that, I did feel him move a bit more with the music. To test the theory Ed suggested we add in a bit of Metallica and Big Wreck as well — just to be sure that Eddie was well rounded. It was an immediate effect — Eddie certainly moved more when the rock music was playing!

It became a nightly routine as my belly grew — Ed sitting on the couch, with my legs over his as I lay beside him. Headphones on my belly as the music played. We gave him one rock song, then classical music, while we watched television. Ed would be able to feel his son the most in those moments, and I felt like we were already a family.

During my pregnancy there were other discoveries and challenges. One of the biggest challenges was my choice of profession.

Growing up, I'd always known that I would one day have children. That, above all else, was a constant goal in my life. I worked hard to go to a good university and obtain a degree that would ensure a career with financial security. The path I chose would lead me to become a Registered Nurse — something that would always ensure I was employed.

By the time my pregnancy rolled around, I was working as a floor nurse, and on my feet for twelve hours straight. As my belly grew, work became more and more difficult. My back was sore, my hips were sore, and my feet were sore. I worked on a heavy floor — heavy in the sense that it was very busy, and the patients were very sick. Heavy in the sense that the patients literally weighed a lot. The floor I worked on was surgical, and many of our surgeries were knee and hip replacements. Patients that needed help standing, transferring, and moving in bed. I was incredibly lucky to have a fantastic team of nurses I worked with, who were always willing to lend a hand — as we all did for each other.

Pregnancy was further complicated when I started retaining water, and my hands and feet swelled. By the time I was six months pregnant, I was no longer able to wear my wedding rings, and I dared not take my shoes off during a shift for fear of my feet swelling and not being able to put them back on. Not wearing my rings caused me added frustration at work as I constantly had patients and their families assume that I was an unwed, knocked up young girl. I was twenty-five years old, but in scrubs and not wearing wedding rings, I did look much younger. There were several times where I was shocked by the nerve of patients and their families — the looks they would give, and the comments they would make. I reasoned that their concerns centered around my youthful appearance, and the need for me to prove that I was educated and capable of caring for their loved one. I understood if they wanted to ensure that only experienced caregivers were involved with their loved ones. For the braver individuals that had the audacity to ask about my pregnancy, I was happy to assure them that I was not only older than they assumed, but also happily married, and yes, my husband was also employed. For the most part, though, this was simply an annoyance. It was easily managed, and I ignored the looks in the beginning, but these looks did cause me a bit of aggravation as my patience wore thin in later months due to my discomfort.

Aside from that, however, being pregnant as a nurse was a wonderful experience. I was able to arrange my schedule to work more night shifts — which allowed me to avoid the fast-paced days and take things at a bit of a slower pace. I was also more than comfortable in the scrubs that were our uniforms — elastic waists are a wonderful thing when your belly is growing. Working the floor, I was also able to wear either running shoes or Crocs — which did help with the swelling and the back pain.

On the floor that I worked, there was a large number of older, more experienced nurses, and I was one of the first new graduates to be placed there. I had previously worked on the floor as a volunteer, and then as a student nurse, so I had established a relationship with most of the staff. I was very fortunate. Many of the older nurses had taken me under their wing, and I looked to many of them as mentors. After I joined the crew, there had been a large influx of new, young nurses.

In the early 2000s, in Canada, there was a mass shortage of qualified nurses. As a university student, choosing my major, I had developed an interest in healthcare, but the idea of securing a career in an industry that was screaming for help also provided the job security I wanted. Once I joined the workforce, there was no shortage of shifts available for me to pick up, and I wanted to work as much as possible to put money away for the future — always planning for the day I became a mother.

Ed and I had met in high school. When we became engaged, we decided to *"work now, play later"* — meaning that we wanted to work as much as possible, and have children young, so that we could travel the world and earn the rewards we dreamed of once we were older. We dreamed of being in our forties and traveling the world. While this was a great idea, it meant that I only socialized with people from work and a few old Niagara friends that Ed had kept in touch with while I was away at school — mostly men.

I had moved out of Niagara for my university years and, being that Facebook and texting did not exist in the late 1990s and early 2000s, there was no simple way to keep in touch with friends from my childhood. We'd all grown up and were living different lives — in various parts of the world. It created an environment where my work friends, who I did hang out with outside of work from time to time, were among the major support systems in my life.

The health system had been reorganizing how they managed staff and opportunities had opened that hadn't been available before. By the time I was pregnant this resulted in an equally large number of nurses in the twenty to forty age range, compared to the older staff. Some of the new girls were young moms and I was able to talk to them about what they had experienced, ask if what I was experiencing was normal, and ask what to expect during the labour and delivery. I was heavily focused during these discussions about labour and delivery. We were a very tight team, and it was a very supportive environment — they even threw me a baby shower. In fact, when I found out I was pregnant, the very first call I made was to one of these nurses — one of my mentors — asking which OB-GYN she would recommend. I spent a considerable amount of time at work, and these relationships were very important to me. They were my friends, as much as coworkers.

Winter turned to spring, and in April, I was thrown two baby showers, one by my family and one by Ed's family. I was seven months pregnant by that time, and my baby bump was big. Not being one that seeks the limelight, I found the showers to be a wonderful, but nerve-wracking experience. I didn't like being the centre of attention, and found it unsettling having so many people wanting to touch my belly. However, I was very appreciative of the gifts that we received and so much love and support being given. Once the second shower was over, I was thrilled to return home and, with Ed, pour over everything we had received — washing, folding, and putting the clothes in the armoire, assembling the crib, putting the mobile in place for the baby to watch.

One of the best things we received was called an AngelCare Monitor. Ed and I had been at odds about where the baby would sleep when we brought him home. Ed wanted the baby in a bassinet at our bedside, but I was absolutely against the baby being in our bedroom.

I had read that having the baby in the bedroom would make the transition to the crib more difficult — the baby would have become used to being soothed by the sound of our own breathing, or the television, and moving him to a crib at an older age would be hard.

Our house was a small bungalow — with our bedroom immediately across the hall from the nursery. At most, Eddie would be sleeping fifty feet from our bed. However, this debate caused the first major disagreement that Ed and I had. We were both absolutely firm in our views. The compromise I had found was the AngelCare Monitor. This device consisted of an audio monitor, which we needed anyways to hear if Eddie was crying, and also a pad that went under the crib mattress and felt for the baby's breaths. An alarm would sound if the baby stopped breathing. Ed was comfortable with that, as was I.

Once, in the middle of the night when Eddie was about four months old, he discovered he could roll — and rolled right off the monitor. I've never in my life seen Ed move as fast as he did when that alarm sounded. He was up, and in the nursery, before I had even registered exactly what was happening. I think Ed's heart had stopped. Eddie, on the other hand, was quite pleased to see Daddy at his bedside, and was grinning a sly little grin. It was the last night we used the AngelCare Monitor.

CHAPTER 5

A t the end of April, about six weeks before my due date, tragedy struck my family. I was standing at my kitchen counter when the reality of what had happened really hit me.

I was cutting an apple with a large kitchen knife and I had been looking out our back window at the orchard our little property bordered on. The sun was high in the clear blue sky, the buds were just forming on the peach trees. It was the beginning of my favourite time of year. Late April and all of May in Niagara are particularly gorgeous times. The chill of the winter is gone, leaving crisp, cool mornings, and hot afternoons. Daffodils, tulips, and hyacinths can be found in gardens and the trees of the orchards are at their most colourful — the bright pink of the cherry trees, and the cool white of the peaches.

It was hard for me to appreciate the beauty though. I had lost my Grandmother just days before. My father's mother, due to a stroke.

As I looked out at the beautiful day, I was suddenly overcome with the magnitude of my loss.

I'd spent the last few days trying to be strong for my family — for my Dad and his sister in particular. The death of a family member impacts each individual in different ways, and grief is something incredibly personal. My grandmother had passed away in the hospital I was working at, two floors down from where I was on shift. I'd not allowed myself the time to really accept what had happened, and grieve myself.

As I cried I felt as if I'd been punched in the gut. The lump in my throat made it hard to speak, let alone breath, and the tears were flowing down my cheeks. It was an ugly cry — the kind where I began gasping for breath, unable to speak. My hands were shaking, and I felt as if my legs were giving out beneath me. Ed was by my side in an instant, taking the knife from my hand and holding me. He allowed me to just cry, and let out my grief.

I was almost eight months pregnant. I was so sad for my loss. I was so sad for the grief that my Dad and his siblings were experiencing. Above all else, I was so incredibly sad for my grandfather, but I didn't know what to *do*. How do you help a person that has lost their partner in life? I was keenly aware that my grandfather was alone for the first time in over 60 years. He had always been there for me, and, although I didn't know what I could do for him, I would be there for him. I began focusing a large amount of time on my grandfather — calling to check in more often, visiting him at the nursing home he lived at more often — just being present. I am a person of action and reaching out made me feel that I was helping in some way.

I had always had a very special relationship with my Dad's parents. I was the first grandchild in the Gale family, and that allowed me a special place in the heart of my grandparents — my grandfather in particular.

Both of my parents are one of the younger siblings in their respective families. This resulted in my having grandparents that seemed older than any of my friends' grandparents, although they would have only been in their early sixties when I was born.

We lived very close to both my maternal and paternal grandparents, but most of my aunts, uncles, and cousins were out of town. My dad's family in particular was dispersed — no other close family in Niagara at all. It meant that my parents were leaned on heavily to support their own parents, in addition to caring for three kids and running a business. The perfect sandwich generation.

I really, truly enjoyed being with my Nanny and Papa Gale. We lived with them for a little while, in the early 1980s — when my parents were building the house I would grow up in. Perhaps this helped to cement the special relationship I had with them. I spent many nights sleeping over at my grandparents' house as a child, and as a teenager I would spend one evening a week with them. We would play cribbage (they let me cheat), ping pong, and watch Toronto Blue Jays games, Jeopardy, and Entertainment Tonight. My grandmother taught me to beat eggs properly (beating with my *wrist*, not my elbow), so that I could help make French toast. Chapmans ice cream, in boxes of course, brings back strong memories of standing in their galley kitchen. They would buy Neapolitan, so that all of us grandchildren would be happy, even though none of us liked the strawberry bits that got on our chocolate or vanilla.

My grandfather was the founder of the family company — a petroleum business that began with heating oil delivery and evolved into gas stations and convenience stores. In my time spent with him he took the opportunity to have many discussions with me about what made a good work ethic, promoting responsibility, and being a reliable employee. He was a great influence on my life, and one of my biggest supporters when I decided to go be a nurse — he was thrilled that I had chosen a profession that would always be in demand.

In the early 1980s my father joined the company, and by the time I was five or six years old I was unofficially working in the office. My father worked long hours — leaving the house before the sun came up, and coming home often after the sun went down. In some ways, he is very similar to my grandfather. I think my connection to both of these men in particular helped to shape who I was to become in adulthood. Strong men, raising a strong woman.

During the particularly impressionable years of my teenage life I was unconsciously developing habits and traits that would form the adult I was to become. I had great conversations with my Dad and my grandfather — learning about struggles my father was having with the company at that time, or the work ethic of my grandfather throughout his life. The best conversations would be in the car, when I'd have one of them for a short period of time in solitude. They were both willing to answer the questions I'd have openly and honestly, never making me feel that any question was silly or out of place. My father still allows me this luxury — and at times, I am able to reciprocate now and answer questions of his own!

As much as I was close to my mother and grandmother as well, it was the men in my life that were the most influential. Even in my friendships I tended to gravitate to males — finding that most males were open, honest, and no drama. If I'd done something to offend them, they let me know, I apologized, and we all moved on. To this day, I continue to surround myself with strong—willed, confident individuals — knowing that I can count on always knowing where I stand with them. I have been fortunate in my adult life to meet other like-minded women, and they form a core group of friends that has supported me through many years.

My father's family is particularly wide-spread. His oldest brother and sister moved to other areas of Ontario, and his other brother moved to the United States — now living in Missouri. It made arranging a wake for my grandmother challenging, and it was eventually scheduled for the first weekend of June that year. Roughly two weeks before my due date.

As much as it was a somber event, the Gale family is one that is always looking to the future — and we all had grieved in our own private ways over the five weeks between her death and her wake. Being able to see all of my aunts, uncles, and cousins — all in one room for the first time in a very long time — was a wonderful thing. Everyone was excited for the birth of my baby — a kind of bright light at the end of a time of great heartache.

CHAPTER 6

For the most part, my pregnancy with Eddie was one of the most wonderful times of my life, but as we grew closer to his arrival I was becoming increasingly worried. I hadn't had a great deal of experience with babies — only after the births of Ed's nieces and nephew. I spoke to as many people as I could — usually the nurses that I was working with.

What should I expect in the delivery room? What should I expect immediately after the baby was born? As Eddie's delivery grew closer, I was focused on the immediate period of during and after birth.

One of my nurse colleagues was the mother of three boys — and all three had been born without any form of pain control. She was extremely proud of this, and I was astonished and very impressed. I was considering various pain relief options that my OB-GYN suggested. He had been advocating for an epidural, which I was not comfortable with. I had a great amount of experience caring for patients with epidurals, and while I knew them to be very safe and incredibly effective, there had always been something about a needle going near my spine that I was very nervous about. The risks were too great, and especially knowing that my friend had birthed three babies with no drugs, I wanted to try to do the same. However, while I did not want to have an epidural during labour, I was not opposed to considering other measures of pain control if needed.

Socially, we were the first of our 'couple' friends to have a baby, and our friends weren't really sure what to do. Coincidentally my closest friend from my university days had her first child three months before Eddie was due — but she was living three hours away. While it was wonderful to have conversations with her, she was hardly a resource I could depend on frequently. As much as everyone was excited for us, they could provide very little advice and support — having never experienced pregnancy or parenthood themselves.

As my due date grew closer, my excitement and nervousness grew. I received a great deal of reassurance that all first time parents were nervous, and we would figure things out as the baby grew. I was told that I should rest up as opportunities for good sleep would be few and far between. I was encouraged to try and breastfeed, as opposed to bottle feeding. I was provided a wide variety of advice, but never once did anyone say anything about my own self-care after the baby was born. Never once did anyone talk to me about mental health, or postpartum depression. Never once did anyone really sit me down and discuss the possible problems that we may face.

I never thought to worry about myself.

I assumed that, as I had been told countless times, whatever happened we would *figure it out.*

My son was due June 19th, 2007. Due to the swelling I suffered from, I chose to begin my maternity leave at the end of May. I was supposed to have a solid four weeks at home, resting up while waiting for the baby to arrive.

It was hot as hell in Niagara by the end of May — temperatures soaring over 90 degrees, and humidity through the roof. Our air conditioning unit was very old, almost as old as I was, and it was having a hard time keeping up during the heatwave. Everything was sticky. It felt like my sweat had sweat. I dressed as minimally as possible — stretchy tank tops, shorts, and my hair in a perpetual ponytail to keep it off my neck. There was little wind to speak of, but even that was hot and provided no relief. The heatwave, along with the added 45 lbs. that I was carrying, made the final weeks leading up to Eddie's birth the most uncomfortable I have ever experienced. To mitigate the heat, I would spend my days in our basement where it was cooler. I carried water bottles filled with ice around the house with me, and a cheap hand fan to try and generate some kind of breeze. Once I started my maternity leave the baby couldn't come fast enough for me. After reaching my 37th week of pregnancy, I breathed easier knowing that Eddie would be safe if he was born. One afternoon, as the temperatures peaked, I looked down at my belly and said, *"Ok, kid, you're fully cooked — now GET OUT!"*

Well, even then, my son was a well-behaved little man who listened to his mama.

Wednesday, June 6th, the final Stanley Cup Playoff of the National Hockey League (NHL) was played — with the Anaheim Mighty Ducks beating the Ottawa Senators. Ed and I were pretty pumped for the game. True Canadians, we are avid hockey fans, particularly minor hockey, but enjoy NHL as well. One of the players on the Anaheim team had played minor hockey for the Niagara Falls Thunder — our local Ontario Hockey League team. We knew the family he had lived with during his days in Niagara, and it was exciting to have even the most remote connection to a potential Stanley Cup winner! Our day was mapped out to ensure that we would be home in time to watch the game.

Ed had worked until 7:00, the morning of June 6th — his last of three night shifts. He was running on only a couple hours of sleep and, as any shiftworker can appreciate, his internal clock was a mess, so he was wide awake come game time. The game started late, as it was being played in California, on the West Coast, and didn't end until close to midnight.

However, before watching the game we had been invited to Ed's brother and sister-in-law's for dinner.

We ordered Chinese Food and the boys went to pick it up in our Toyota Rav4. The restaurant was only a few minutes from their house. I had been chatting with my sister-in-law, Jackie, when the phone rang.

Jackie picked up the phone, and I could tell something was wrong, instantly! She looked at me, then turned slightly away while saying:

"Ok. Ok. Uh huh. Yup, no problem. Keep me posted," she said, then hung up.

Jackie stared back at me, sighed, rolled her eyes, and said: *"Well, you're never going to believe this. The boys were on their way back from the restaurant, stopped at a set of lights, and some guy backed out of his driveway right into the Rav."*

My jaw dropped. *WHAT?!* Our new SUV, bought only last fall, was supposed to be our primary mode of transportation for the baby. We had already installed the car seat base and everything — just to be sure we were ready.

In that moment, my temper got the better of me, and I was up out of my chair in a moment, trying to put my shoes on. I was hell bent on driving to the scene of the accident to give the offender a piece of my mind until I realized that I had no vehicle to get there in. Jackie was trying to keep me calm, and managed to talk some sense into me — reasoning that showing up there would not help the situation.

35

An hour later, after the police had written their report and the men had exchanged insurance information, the boys returned with the Chinese food — now cold and soggy. I waddled outside and looked at the Rav.

The back passenger door was caved in. So much so that we couldn't even open the door. This caused a larger problem being that the car seat base was installed on that side of the seat. I was fuming — "*how could this happen?!,*" I yelled. We were days away from having a baby, this is certainly NOT what we needed to deal with right now.

Ed explained that it had been an elderly man who backed right out of his driveway, directly into the car. Ed had been at a dead stop. The man had admitted he hadn't even looked in his rearview mirror. I was so angry, I could barely see straight.

"*What an absolute moron!*" I said.

"*Yes, the officer said something more politically correct but along the same lines as well,*" Ed said. "*There was absolutely no reason for this to have happened,*" he added.

We ate quickly and went home. I was so upset my stomach was in knots. Ed was exhausted from lack of sleep, and miserable due to the accident and my emotional state. All we wanted was to go home, watch the hockey game, and go to bed. We could deal with the car in the morning.

There was one last job we needed to do before settling down to watch the hockey game. The next day was garbage day and putting the garbage out the night before was standard practice for all of us in our neighbourhood. We diligently collected our garbage and placed it at the end of our driveway the night before.

As the game ended, and midnight passed, sleep came slowly. It was short-lived, and I awoke in terror at 2:00 a.m., to the sound of gunshots coming down the road. Ed woke up too, perhaps to my scream, perhaps to the gunshots. Just as quickly as they started though, they vanished.

We both went to the window in the nursery, where we could look out to the road, and saw garbage everywhere. We quickly realized that the gunshots were really the sounds of garbage cans being hit by baseball bats as a car was driving by — called 'garbage can baseball' and a game that local teenagers had been known to take part in. Realizing that neither of us were going to be settling back to sleep we grabbed two flashlights, turned on the house lights, and went outside to clean up the mess.

Ed tried to tell me to stay in the house — he could handle the clean up, but I was wide awake and wanting to help. I attempted to pick up an item or two, but my belly was so big that I was scared of losing my balance and landing on my head. Ed just rolled his eyes at me, heaved a big sigh and asked me to stop moving. Muttering under his breath he put me in charge of holding both flashlights, as he cleaned up the yard. I'm sure I wasn't being much help.

At that moment, something inside of me cracked. I suddenly realized just how ridiculous the last twelve hours had been. Me, nine months pregnant, sausage fingers and toes, no wedding rings, no shoes that would fit (thank God for Crocs!); a car accident hours earlier, a husband that was absolutely miserable, and now picking up trash in the dark at 2:00 a.m.!!! I lost it. I started laughing. I mean, I started *howling!!* Doubled over, trying not to fall. It was the only reaction that I could come up with at the time. I couldn't hold the flashlight still — which didn't help with Ed's mood. He became increasingly frustrated with my loss of sanity very quickly.

Then it happened. Deep in my belly I felt a pop. *"Oh, no, is this it?"* I asked myself.

That sobered me up pretty quickly. I didn't say anything to Ed, just appeared to regain my grip on reality and actually be of assistance with the flashlight. We finished up, and went inside. I went to the washroom and quickly realized that we weren't going to be getting any more sleep right then.

I walked into the bedroom, where Ed was just laying back down, and stood at the foot of the bed.

He looked at me, and rolled his eyes, *'What's wrong now?'* he asked.

I twiddled my fingers for a second, took a deep breath and then informed my exhausted, frustrated, weary, wonderful husband that we needed to get to the hospital. My water had broken and it was time to have a baby.

As nervous and excited as I was, it didn't hold a candle to the way that Ed reacted. He jumped out of bed, throwing clothes on, grabbing the diaper bag, and rushing to the car. He came running back for me, helping me put on my shoes, double checking that we had everything we thought we would need, and guiding me to the car.

Off to the hospital we went. By 3:00 a.m., I was hooked up to more monitors than I cared to acknowledge. To my dismay, it was determined I was not in active labour yet — but the nurses verified that my water had definitely broken. I was the only woman in the maternity ward at that time. This, coupled with the fact that I had mentioned I was a nurse at the same hospital, prompted the nurses to let me stay — reasoning that I'd be back within hours anyways.

I was thrilled! It was time. My baby boy was coming.

Slowly. He was coming slowly.

The kid certainly took his time. That day reminds me of the episode on Friends when Rachel is having her baby — there were two or three women who came in and birthed their children while I twiddled my fingers.

The first ten hours of my labour were unremarkable and I did not see my doctor until the early afternoon. I was worried that my labour was not progressing, and that he may send me home until I was having stronger, more consistent contractions. I did not want to go home. I wanted this to be the day I met my son. Up to the point that my doctor visited, I would have an occasional contraction — a slight twinge through my abdomen that really felt no worse than a menstrual cramp. There was no regularity to the timing of the contractions.

While I knew that delivering a baby could take a significant amount of time, actually being the woman in labour was much more frustrating than I had expected it to be. It seemed like all I was doing was sitting in a bed, twiddling my thumbs. It was difficult not to become increasingly frustrated at what I envisioned was a lack of progressing through labour. While I pestered the nurses with questions about how far along I was, they really couldn't answer my questions without the doctor arriving to perform a proper exam. I had been waiting *nine months* to meet my baby — where was the doctor!? Didn't he know how important today was?? I am not a patient person. All I wanted was to meet my son, and I was ready!!

At 1:00 p.m., my doctor came to visit me. Upon examination, he assured me that, despite the irregular contractions, my body was progressing and preparing itself for the baby to be born. As it had already been eleven hours since my water broke he would not send me home. Instead, he laid out two options: One, to wait a few more hours and see if the contractions become more regular. Two, to be induced. I learned that not only had my water broken, but they had found meconium in the fluid — indicating that the baby had defecated in utero (lovely, by the way, I was *thrilled* to hear that — ew!). Either way, they would induce me as there was a risk to the baby due to the meconium. Meconium is essentially the first stool of a baby. Most babies pass the meconium after they are born, but some do so before. It was explained to me that the meconium could cause lung infections in newborns, and they would need to take measures to avoid this — one of those measures being to ensure his imminent birth.

The decision was an easy one, and I quickly elected to be induced as soon as possible. My patience was further tested when it took another hour for the induction to begin. By that time, my mother and sister were there. As the oldest of the family, I was close to both my younger brother, Bobby, and sister, Angela. There were almost five years gap between me and Angie, which was a world of difference as children, but

38

as grown ups, we had developed a great sense of respect for each other. She was now in university herself, and while we didn't see each other often we spoke regularly. The school year had finished in April, and we had been able to spend a significant amount of time together the last six weeks. This was going to be her first nephew, and she was incredibly excited to meet him.

I had asked for Angie and my mom to be at the hospital, to help pass the time and support me while waiting for Eddie to arrive. However, the plan was that once I started pushing, only Ed would be in the room with me. They helped during the early part of my labour as Ed and I passed the time. It was wonderful to have them there. We spent the time talking and laughing, each of us giddy at the thought of a new baby.

The medication that was used to start the induction was administered through my IV. As I lay in the hospital bed, I wasn't convinced the induction was working — the contractions still felt like nothing more than menstrual cramps. I was too excited to relax and sleep, but I was becoming more and more tired. I hadn't had more than two hours of sleep in the past 36 hours, thanks to the excitement of the day before. Since entering the hospital, I hadn't been allowed to eat anything more than ice chips, in case a cesarean section was required. Tired, hungry, and becoming more anxious as the day went on. I'm sure I was not the easiest patient although the nurses were really lovely.

I had received a great deal of fluids through the IV and what goes in must come out, as they say. There came a point when I felt the need to use the washroom. I took my trusty IV pole, and Ed walked with me to the washroom, which was found just outside of my delivery room in the hallway. I did my business, washed my hands, and opened the door to journey back to the delivery room.

I took a step, and a tremor ran through my abdomen from my back, around both of my sides, and meeting in the centre of my belly. It felt like my abdomen was being split open. My legs were suddenly dangerously weak and I feared they would give out. My field of vision spun, and I felt like I was going to pass out. I gasped, and grabbed Ed's arm. For a minute, I couldn't move, then, I couldn't get back to bed fast enough. My mom and sister took one look at my face as I entered the room and knew something had changed. Ed called for the nurse and that was the last time I saw my mom and sister before delivering my son.

That bathroom venture had occurred around 5:00 p.m., and by 6:00 p.m., I was begging for pain control. During that hour the contractions that had been weak and irregular were suddenly incredibly intense and frequent. Only minutes between each one. I tried to breathe evenly and deeply, but the long day was catching up with me. I was weak due to no food and no sleep. I was beside myself and needed something to bring relief. The alternative suggested to me was an injection in my leg of Demerol.

It was my first time ever having Demerol. It was also my last.

The injection was given in my leg and within minutes I was reacting to the drug. I vomited violently, and started hallucinating. I was on my back, on the bed, and it seemed that there were dozens of people around me — faces fading in and out of my view. The world had taken on a strange, dreamlike quality. It didn't seem real, as if I was watching what was happening in the room as a spectator, not an active participant. The pain had been dulled, but was not gone. I had lost the strength in my arms and legs. I couldn't raise my head to look to the end of the bed.

My perception of time became skewed. I wasn't sure how long I'd been in labour for, or how long it had been since I'd had the Demerol. When it came time I wasn't lucid enough to gather the strength required to push properly. The nurses seemed frustrated, and appeared to be shouting at me to push. It was hard to focus on what they were saying. I bore down as best I could, but could not put any power behind what I was trying to do. My baby was being born and *I was missing it*.

At 8:54 p.m. on June 7th, 2007, I gave birth to Edward Robert John Friesen. 7lbs., 14 oz. of perfection. Or so I was told.

I was not aware of the actual moment of birth. Suddenly, Ed was by my side confirming it was a boy. He confirmed that there were ten fingers and ten toes. I did not see my baby from any closer than the opposite end of the bed. Even then, he was a blur, and then my baby was taken away from me.

I started crying — sobbing, uncontrollably. The Demerol was still affecting my consciousness. I couldn't stop long enough to explain why I was crying, and asking myself, *"where was my baby??"* Looking back, I'm sure that no one really understood what was happening with me at that moment. The nurse looked at me like I'd lost my mind. She asked why I was crying, and I couldn't put the words together. They had probably explained what was happening with my son, but in my skewed reality I could not understand where he was. I only knew that he was not with me.

My son had been taken to the Neonatal Intensive Care Unit (NICU), as a precaution due to the meconium. Once the Demerol wore off, closer to 10:30 p.m., it was explained that he had gone there for monitoring and antibiotic treatment — just in case he had swallowed any of the meconium into his lungs. I was assured this was standard procedure, no big deal.

It's funny what stands out in the moments of lucidity. As the Demerol wore off, I realized I was *starving*. Of course I was! I hadn't eaten anything more than ice chips in 24 hours! I started making sense of my surroundings around 10:30 at night. It was then that I asked Ed to go get me a Wendy's hamburger (single burger, no tomatoes, no pickles STAT!). By this time, my mom and sister had left. I was moved to a postpartum patient room, and encouraged to close my eyes and rest. Eddie was in the best place possible, and the NICU nurses were taking care of him. There was nothing more for me to do at that time.

CHAPTER 7

The Greater Niagara General Hospital had opened in the mid-1950s and the maternity department was situated on the ground floor. The delivery area, NICU, and postpartum area were all in one wing. In 2007, every mother was provided a private room in the postpartum area, even though the rooms were actually standard patient rooms that would typically hold two beds. First-time parents were allowed to have their spouse join them in the room overnight.

I woke up at 2:00 a.m. on June 8th, frantic. I had to take a moment and reorient myself. My entire body felt sore, and I had a horrible headache. My belly was soft. I could see Ed curled up on the recliner in the corner of the room but there was no baby in the room.

"Where was my son? What was going on?" Questions I was asking myself.

The Demerol had worn off, and I was desperately trying to piece together the events of the past few hours.

Fragments of the evening before started coming back slowly, and I remembered that Eddie had been taken to the NICU. A thousand questions were going through my mind. I tried to sit up quickly and was hit by a wave of vertigo. I laid back down, as I held my head to try and stop the spinning. Quickly, I did a full body scan — the strength had returned to my legs and arms, and as I felt my soft belly I started panicking.

Oh, how had this happened? How bad was this? Tears sprung to my eyes, as confusion set into my mind. Suddenly all my years of nursing school were kicking in. Antibiotic treatment due to meconium was certainly not rare, but also certainly not typical. Something was wrong with my baby, and mama bear was waking from hibernation.

I sat up slowly and rose to my feet. My slippers were beside the bed, and I put them on to protect my feet from the cold floor. I slowly walked over and woke Ed up. Wiping sleep out of his own eyes, exhausted in his own right, he went to the hallway to find a wheelchair. He helped me sit down in it, and wheeled me through the maze of halls to take me to Eddie.

To enter the NICU, we needed to don gowns, gloves, and masks. Having to do this increased my anxiety twofold. First, because it increased my alarm that something serious was wrong with my son and no one was telling me. Second, because it delayed me meeting my son, and knowing there was only one more door between him and I was almost too much for me to accept.

Finally, I was wheeled into the room. There, to my right, was what I can only describe as a type of incubator. It was open at the top, with a type of heat lamp shining down, and clear plexiglass walls on the sides so that nothing could fall out.

In this tiny incubator with far too many wires and monitors, was my precious baby boy. He was asleep in a tiny diaper, his arms and legs splayed wide. I was not allowed to pick him up. He was five hours old, and I had not yet held my son. It was reassuring to see for myself the ten tiny fingers and ten tiny toes. There was a very fine, almost translucent dusting of downy hair on the top of his head. He had chubby cheeks, and a tiny nose. He looked absolutely perfect and peaceful. I felt my heart settle to be able to see him, and know where he was.

Now, finally, with my wits about me, I was able to ask for information on a more technical level than had been provided earlier in the night. The NICU nurse recognized that I had not been provided all of the information the night before. She explained, *"yes, Eddie was in the NICU due to the meconium, however, it was more serious than that. Eddie was in the NICU because his blood oxygen levels had been so low when he was born. He needed to be monitored through the night in order to ensure there was no serious damage."*

I knew what she was saying to me. There was a chance Eddie had been born with Cerebral Palsy — a brain injury commonly caused by lack of oxygen during the birth process. In Eddie's case, this possibility was in direct correlation to the Demerol I had chosen to be injected with only a few hours before his birth. I had taken great care to prepare my body for a baby before conception, then taken good care of my son in my womb for nine months, and one decision in the final moments of pregnancy may have changed his life forever. The pain I felt in my chest was crushing, making it hard to breathe. I was absolutely shattered but I couldn't let on. I said nothing to Ed, but stoically maintained a straight face. I had to remain calm, so that Ed remained calm. As I looked down at my perfect son, it seemed a cruel joke that the first decision I'd made as a mother could have gone so horribly wrong.

How could I tell my husband that my decision had almost killed our baby? I felt cold, as I felt guilty.

This had to be a dream. There was no way this was real. It took every ounce of strength to keep myself together.

What could I do? 'What's done was done,' as they say. I looked at my baby boy knowing that I had a host of questions that the nurse couldn't answer for me. I had to wait for the doctor, and remained as calm as possible so that I didn't scare my husband.

My son was less than twelve hours old and I had already failed him.

———

We did not stay in the NICU for long. Eddie was sleeping, and Ed and I were both exhausted. Ed wheeled me back to my postpartum room and we resumed our previous sleeping arrangements. Soon, I could hear Ed's soft breathing — he had fallen asleep almost immediately.

I spent the night staring at the ceiling of my hospital room, listening to the nurses chatting at the nearby nurses station, hearing newborn babies crying from other rooms. I could hear footsteps of another mother who seemed to be pacing — possibly trying to soothe her newborn to sleep. That's what I should have been doing — holding my son and soothing him on his first night in this world. Instead, Ed was in a recliner, and I was twenty feet away, alone in a hospital bed. Our son was in a room, all alone, with no one to hold him. The warmth he was feeling was not from

45

his mother, but from a heat lamp. He was not sleeping in my arms, or in the bassinet beside me, but on a table — as if he was a piece of meat. My heart was breaking as I went over the events of the night before. Everything had been okay up to the point where I took the Demerol. Tears came to my eyes as I accepted that I simply hadn't been strong enough to birth my son without pain control. My weakness had won, and my son would be the victim of his mother's poor decision.

I have always believed that a mother's job was to make the best decision for their child with the information they have at that time...and that mothers were not able to make 'wrong' decisions if the decisions were made with their child's best interest at heart. That night, staring at the ceiling, I felt that I was being punished because I had put my needs in front of my sons. I had chosen to mitigate my pain, rather than consider what the risks were for my baby with the method of pain control I chose. I was totally consumed thinking that I had risked my son's life, just as it was about to begin.

Taking the Demerol is one of the worst decisions of my life. It took me years to realize that there was no way to know that I would react to Demerol so badly.

Sleep was not to be my friend that night and by 8:00 a.m., I was back in the NICU. Ed and I had eaten a quick breakfast and then rushed to be by our son. From my time as a nurse, I knew that there was typically no rhyme or reason to the times that doctors did their rounds. I desperately needed to speak to the NICU doctor, I need to learn what was really happening. My imagination was quickly running away with me, and my anxiety was rising again.

This time, donned in gown, glove, and mask, upon entering the NICU, I saw that Eddie had been moved to a small enclosure. He was still in only a diaper, with the heat lamp, but had fewer wires and the IV was not hooked up. He was again sleeping, his head turned to his left side, and there were small mittens on his hands to prevent his nails from scratching him. I sat beside him, just staring. I was scared to touch him, and possibly hurt him again. The nurse on duty smiled at me, and asked, *"would you like to hold him."* I was terrified, but I very much wanted to hold the little boy that was all mine.

As Eddie had now received his first dose of antibiotic, I was allowed to remove my gloves and my mask. The nurse opened the enclosure, carefully lifted Eddie out of it, and placed him in my arms.

Relief and gratitude filled my heart instantly. I was so grateful to be able to hold Eddie — as if just being able to touch him made him real. Finally, something was going right. No one should have to be separated from their child immediately after birth. I only experienced that for a few hours — I can't imagine the sheer terror a parent would feel if they were separated from their baby for days. I could feel his heartbeat, and see his chest evenly rising and falling. He had long eyelashes and managed a fierce grip on my thumb. Sitting, holding my son, I was overcome by the feeling of relief. I could see for myself that he had ten fingers and ten toes. He looked so perfect, like a tiny doll. As relieved as I was, I was equally terrified. I had already hurt him once, and I didn't know how much he would suffer for my poor decision making. I didn't trust myself not to hurt him again.

Looking at my son, and how perfect he appeared, it was hard to wrap my mind around what I feared his reality may be, based on my poor decision. I knew firsthand how *Cerebral Palsy* could manifest.

As a nursing student, I had worked for a company that provided respite care for families. This was mostly to provide an individual's primary caregivers with a much-needed break. I did whatever the family needed me to do. During that time, I had two cases that were children with Cerebral Palsy.

One was a girl, about thirteen years old. She was wheelchair bound, not able to control her arms and legs, and was unable to speak. She was an absolute sweetheart who enjoyed Capris Sun drinks and watermelon cubes. I would spend two hours with her a week, giving her a bath, feeding her an evening snack, and tucking her in bed.

The second was a young man in his early twenties. He was able to control his limbs, and he could walk. He was not able to speak and had to wear a hockey helmet, because he was prone to seizures that would cause him to fall suddenly. The helmet was to prevent any major head injuries, and he wore it from the moment he woke up, to the moment he went to bed. He liked bagels with cream cheese and watching Saturday morning cartoons with me. I was with him for four hours every Saturday morning. I would help him get dressed, help him eat breakfast, and watch TV, or play with some toys.

As I held my baby boy in my arms, I could see both of the latter individuals' faces. I could see their parents faces, and the constant concern that they lived with. Would this be our reality? As I reflected, I was terrified to know the answer.

A few hours later, the pediatrician made rounds and assured me that Eddie would be just fine, and not to give it another thought. *"The oxygen deprivation had not been severe enough, for long enough, to cause any serious lasting effects,"* he said, and further reassured me by pointing that out. Although, the fact that Eddie was not receiving oxygen in the enclosure, was a detail I had missed.

My son was safe. My son was healthy. My son was not going to be permanently damaged by my foolish decision to put my needs above his. I would not have to face my family and friends knowing that I was the cause of my son's struggles. I would not have to live with the fear that my husband would resent me because of the decision I'd made that had impacted our child so severely. I would not have to, one day admit to Eddie himself, that my foolishness had ruined his life. He would be okay.

However, something in me had been broken during the last twenty-four hours.

To this day, I do not know if there is one 'thing' that can be blamed for the lack of bonding that occurred between Eddie and I at that time. I spoke to other mothers and heard of the immediate all-powerful, crushing love they felt for their baby the moment the baby was placed in their arms.

In the hospital, in my son's first few days of life, after the relief of realizing that he was not going to suffer due to my inexperience, I felt nothing more for my son. No love, no hatred, no resentment — just a vast, black, void of *nothing*. I didn't realize yet that the excitement, love, and hope I had known while pregnant was gone — replaced by fear. Fear that the worst thing for my baby might actually be ME. In those first days I just knew that I was scared, exhausted, and still in considerable pain. I was supposed to care for this baby — and that meant ensuring that he was cleaned, clothed, and fed. I could manage those three things.

We stayed in the hospital a total of three nights. The first two nights, Eddie was in the NICU. During that time, only two people were allowed to enter the NICU at a time. It was a sort of surreal quasi-motherhood. I was visiting my baby. If I happened to be there when he needed his diaper changed, I was permitted to do so — other times the nurses would change him. I was expected to be there every two hours, in order to attempt to breastfeed. Otherwise, the NICU was really very small and became crowded quickly. The nurses were efficient and knew exactly what was needed. While they were very helpful, I was consistently encouraged to return to my room to rest, making me feel unwelcome there.

Eddie had been born on a Thursday. On Saturday morning, after being visited by the on-duty pediatrician, Eddie graduated out of the NICU and into my room. We were to spend one more night in the hospital. The next morning, if everything went well, we would be going home. That day, and into the early evening, there was a constant flow of visitors in my hospital room. Family, friends, and coworkers came to meet Eddie and express their excitement. It was an overwhelming time of excitement for everyone — except for me. My trepidation at being discharged was easy to hide with so many people all wanting to congratulate me. Everyone was very ginger with me — expecting me to still be sore from the birth and reading the lines on my face to be from exhaustion alone.

That evening, Ed went home for a few hours. To shower, to prepare the house, to do whatever he felt needed to be done for his son to come home. For the first time ever, Eddie and I were absolutely alone. I lay in my hospital bed looking at Eddie in the bassinet. In that hospital room, behind a closed door, I was suddenly scared of the tiny little baby beside me. My thoughts were, *what if he cried and I couldn't soothe him? What if he wouldn't eat? What if he wouldn't sleep? Here, I am surrounded by people that could help him. But soon, we would have to go home. Who would protect my son from me there?*

CHAPTER 8

Eddie and I came home on the morning of Sunday, June 10th, 2007 — one year to the day after our wedding. It was a gorgeous day. The heat wave was still going, the sun was shining in the cloudless blue sky, and our baby was healthy. It should have been a spectacular moment.

Instead, as we left the hospital, I felt a knot forming in the pit of my stomach. I was a responsible, capable adult. I had planned for motherhood my entire life; all of my decisions had been in preparation for this moment. However, while leaving the hospital and the nurses there that assisted me, reality was setting in. I had no idea what to do with a baby. I'd never really handled a baby before. I had been so focused on the pregnancy, and preparing for the birth, that I had never thought about what it would be like to *live* with a baby.

The Greater Niagara General Hospital is situated at the corner of Portage Road and North Street in Niagara Falls. Close enough to the old downtown that transients can be found regularly up and down the surrounding roadways. There are bars and pawn shops where, those that need to, can sell their possessions to finance their next pack of cigarettes or whatever their pleasure may be. The hospital emergency room was often full of those less fortunate — coming to the ER to seek help or just a warm place for the night. My heart had always gone out to them — individuals that had not been as fortunate as me. Those that had been born into a hard life, or who had made decisions that lead to a hard life.

As we drove up North Street away from the hospital, one of these people, a man, was at the side of the road. He had long, scraggly hair, and sunburnt skin. Wearing old flip-flops, dirty jeans, and a t-shirt with holes in it. He was pushing a grocery buggy, with what I could only imagine, were all his worldly possessions in them. A cigarette was balanced carefully on his lip, and he had a bottle of some kind of booze on the top of the buggy. As we drove by, for a moment, he looked up, and our eyes met.

My heart broke for him, and tears sprang to my eyes. I thought of the hopes and dreams that I believed his mother would have had for him when he was born. At that moment, I thought of all the people in that man's life that should have been there for him. All the people that were put in charge of ensuring he felt safe and secure, had food to eat, a warm bed, and the opportunity to thrive. All of the people that had somehow failed him. This man was a lost soul. *Was this man a victim of his own poor decisions, that others couldn't save him from? Or was he a victim of 'the system' — not receiving the help he needed?* It didn't matter. In a split second my heart absolutely broke for him, and I thought of my own baby boy sitting just behind me in his car seat — and I knew that I would do everything possible to ensure that he was put on the right track in life. I would do everything possible to ensure that he was never lost.

I would make sure that my son was ready for whatever life threw at him. *But how?*

The hospital had provided me with a discharge package that included a variety of pamphlets on different programs offered to assist new parents. My first task upon returning home was to peruse the pamphlets and see what services were available, if I needed them. Many of the programs revolved around the Ontario Early Years Centre, which operated closest to our house, out of one of the Catholic Elementary Schools in Niagara Falls. There were programs for babies starting when they were newborn, and I quickly figured out which ones I could take part in. Being the second week of June, most of the programs were just finishing and I would have to wait until the beginning of July to start the first one.

This worked out well for us, as Ed had arranged to be home for the first three weeks after Eddie was born. To spend those precious days helping with Eddie and adjusting to our new life.

That afternoon, after taking time to pour through the rest of the pamphlets and completing whatever paperwork was necessary, I was at a loss of what to do. I stumbled through that first afternoon. I had previously lived a life that was carefully orchestrated. At work, I had any number of tasks to be completed, all, at the direction of doctors' orders. At home, my days were filled with tasks that I felt were necessary. Now, I had nothing but time ahead of me for the next year to stay at home, take care of my baby, and adjust to life as a family of three. For the first time in my life, I was without a schedule. While I'm sure many people would revel in the new found freedom, I was totally lost. There was no guidebook telling me what to do day to day. I began quickly spiralling, feeling out of control.

I needed the world to stop. I needed someone to guide me. I needed someone to say, *'Your job right now is to love your baby, and snuggle him, and take care of yourself — and everything else will fall into place.'* I am very good at putting on a brave face though, and I spoke of this to absolutely no one. At the time, I felt it was a badge of honour to never let anyone know I was scared, confused, and feeling out of control. I had already failed my son once — I was not going to let anyone know I was scared of doing so again!

All I could plan around was knowing that, every two hours, Eddie would be hungry. I was struggling trying to breastfeed him. I knew that bottle feeding was a solid alternative, but I also felt a considerable amount of pressure from women around me to breastfeed. Additionally, I put a significant amount of pressure on myself to breastfeed. In my mind, if I could not breastfeed, it was one more way that I was failing my son.

In the hours since returning home, Eddie and I just couldn't get the knack of breastfeeding! I learned years later that another possible side effect of using Demerol for pain control was the infant being slow to pick up breastfeeding. At the hospital, there had always been a nurse present to help me get him latched. Now, alone at home, Eddie was crying and all I knew was that he was hungry, and I was in pain.

As I sat on our couch, with Eddie in my lap, tearfully trying to 'figure it out', Ed was pouring through the paraphernalia that we had been provided by the hospital. He came upon a pamphlet for MotherRisk — a 24-hour helpline that was available to answer any questions that parents could think to ask. Hoping that they would be able to give some helpful tips, I quickly called them. I explained my struggle, and asked if I should consider giving him a bottle if this struggle continued much longer.

What I received was a lecture on how 'Breast is Best,' and I shouldn't even consider switching to a bottle because *if* I were to do that *and* try nursing as well, it would cause 'nipple confusion' — and that would be traumatic for the baby.

I should remind the reader that this was in 2007. Yes, the internet was around, and yes, I could have used it to gain more information. But, at this time, I wasn't as internet-savvy as I am now. 2007 was the year the first iPhone was introduced! A smartphone was only something I had heard of, not actually used. I had been raised to trust my doctor. Even though I was a healthcare professional myself, all of my instincts were thrown out the window when I became a mother — I did not trust myself. I had to trust others. I had to trust the professionals that I was surrounded by.

In the span of a five-minute phone call, the nurse from MotherRisk had alarmed me so completely about the possibility of 'nipple confusion' that I decided to breastfeed exclusively. This phone call resulted in Eddie being strictly breastfed for the first three months of his life — chaining me to my son completely, and making me feel that I had narrowly avoided failing him again. At that time, the afternoon I brought him home, all I knew was, I would figure out this breastfeeding thing somehow. The nurse encouraged me to call the Ontario Early Years Centre (OEYC) as they offered breastfeeding assistance — I could go to the centre and be assessed.

Desperate for help, I called the OEYC and made an appointment for the next day.

As I hung up the phone, I stared at Eddie in the crook of my left arm, and the wireless receiver I held in my right arm. My hand started shaking, tears were flooding my eyes, and I couldn't see anymore. There were stars appearing in my vision, and my head started spinning. Ed saw me starting to cry and quickly took Eddie from me and sat me on the couch. My breathing was becoming erratic, coming in quick gasps. I was having a panic attack. My hearing was suddenly muffled. Sounds seeming to be coming from far away. I lay on the couch, closed my eyes, and willed the world to stop.

Ed didn't know what to do. He didn't know I couldn't see, he didn't know I couldn't hear. He just knew that I was crying. He was holding his son, and watching as his wife fell apart.

He asked me what I needed.

"My Mom," was all I could say.

Bright and early the next morning, we packed Eddie up and made our way to the Ontario Early Years Centre in Niagara Falls — to the breastfeeding clinic. Eddie and I had struggled through the night trying to breastfeed, but it just didn't seem to be working. I was in a great amount of pain from the milk that was coming in, and Eddie was having a hard time latching and filling his tummy.

Our first night at home had been challenging. Eddie had been up at least every two hours to try and eat. Between feeding attempts Ed and I had slept lightly, both of us keeping one ear open in case Eddie began to start crying. Come morning we were both exhausted.

The last thing on my mind as we left the house was my appearance, so my hair was put in a ponytail, my face make-up free, and my trusted yoga pants were on. Ed was only marginally better — having been able to accomplish getting a shower that morning. We must have been quite a sight.

When we arrived at the OEYC, we saw another couple leaving just as we were entering the centre. To my surprise, Ed gave a friendly wave to the man and stopped to chat. I realized that they looked vaguely familiar — they had been in the NICU with their newborn at the same time as we were there with Eddie. I was introduced to Jack, his wife Mary, and their newborn son Evan. They were first time parents as well. Ed and Jack had chatted in the NICU, but while I had seen Mary there, she and I had not met each other. We were roughly the same age, both our boys had minor complications at birth, and now we were both struggling at home. While I wasn't in the mood for an unplanned conversation right at that moment, I smiled, and the men exchanged phone numbers. It was agreed that, once we were all settled, we would reach out and see about getting together sometime. I was hesitantly optimistic that these were good people, and that we would be able to support each other as we navigated being new parents. It was nice to meet another new mom, and possibly someone I could talk to about my struggles.

The consultant at the OEYC was very kind. Unlike the nurse from MotherRisk, she encouraged me to keep trying to breastfeed but tried to assure me that bottle-feeding was a great option as well. She was the first person who seemed to see how stressed I was with little Eddie. She took the time to talk to me about how I was struggling with breastfeeding. Furthermore, she stated that the most important thing was to ensure that Eddie was eating — and it didn't matter if he ate formula or breastmilk. She offered a few suggestions to make my breastfeeding attempts easier — tips on how to hold Eddie, how to position myself with pillows, etc. I felt that I had been given a few tools that would assist me and Eddie, but her reassurance that 'nipple confusion' would not occur, did little to placate me. I was scared that if I couldn't figure out breastfeeding, and had to bottle feed only, I would have failed as a mother again.

CHAPTER 9

Those precious first few weeks should have been a time to enjoy adjusting to having Eddie home. Ed was home and everything should have been that much easier with him there. Ed would never balk at any job. Diapers, bathing, tending a crying baby — nothing phased him. The one thing he couldn't help with was feeding.

Instead, Eddie's first few days at the hospital and the phone call with MotherRisk had terrified me so completely that I was scared to be alone with my son. I would not even discuss providing Eddie a bottle, for fear that he would then not breastfeed. He was a slow eater, and it was nothing for a feeding to last forty-five minutes. The length of his feedings, and frequency of his feeding caused an extreme amount of added pressure. No matter how wonderful Ed was with the baby, I was constantly needed to feed Eddie — there was no break for me, and no end in sight. It felt like a rollercoaster that I couldn't get off of, or like I was drowning and unable to be able to come up for air. There was no respite.

Our first evening home, after my first-ever panic attack, Ed had fulfilled my wish and taken me to see my mother. We had driven quickly to my parents' house, spent an hour or two there, and gone home. This event had established a ritual that I would depend upon for the first few days after bringing Eddie home, as well as periodically throughout that summer.

In the hospital, the very first time Eddie and I had been alone in my room together, I had been terrified. Terrified that I, the person who was supposed to protect this tiny little helpless baby, was actually the person that was the most dangerous for him. The anxiety that I first felt in that moment had become like a parasite in my life. I began living with a constant undercurrent of anxiety in my gut. It felt like I was operating with a constant 'humming' of anxiety — like an electrical transformer just waiting to explode. As the day went on, my anxiety would grow stronger — the knot building in my belly, my hands shaking, pressure building in my chest until it was hard to breath, and my pulse would race. Finally, it would begin to affect my vision and my mind would begin to run wild. I would not be able to focus on anything. Inside I was screaming that I simply needed everything to just STOP.

The only thing that would make my anxiety recede was to see my mother. She was an individual I trusted. It didn't need to be for a long time — half an hour would do. Just long enough that I could breathe again. Just long enough that the pressure in my chest and the knot in my stomach would loosen slightly. Just long enough for my heart rate to calm, and my vision to clear, and we would go home. Every night for the first week, just after dinner I would be an emotional wreck. I needed to know that I wasn't alone, and a hug from my mom was like a wave of calm washing over me. I never explained to my parents or Ed why I wanted to visit. My parents were thrilled that they got to see their first grandchild, and Ed was thrilled that I seemed calmer whenever we would head back home. This, in addition to the MotherRisk phone call and breastfeeding challenges, made the first few days of Eddie being home almost unbearable. I almost regretted that I had ever wanted to be a mother. I just kept thinking, *what have I done to my life? What have I done to Eddie's life?* The regret, fear, and shame only added to the anxiety, and this became a vicious circle of negative thoughts that would suck me deeper and deeper into my depression as the days went on.

———————

In the days following our arrival home, I quickly lost track of time and was aware of only when Eddie had last eaten, and when he was due to eat again. I felt like a cow — constantly being milked. My body did not feel like my own. The knot in my stomach that had developed when leaving the hospital was a constant companion. I was emotional — crying at the drop of a hat, lashing out in anger if something wasn't just perfect in my eyes. My hormones were running wild. It never occurred to me that this was not the way a new mother should feel.

We had visitors every day, sometimes multiple times a day. No one ever questioned my behaviour. Everyone focused on Eddie, asking how he was adapting to be home. No one ever truly asked how Ed and I were adapting to being parents in more than just a flippant, polite question. The kind of rhetorical question that expects an answer of, *"tired, but we're okay."*

While it was wonderful to see everyone, it did make it very difficult to establish any type of routine with Eddie outside of his feedings. I felt that there was no time to just sit and figure out how to be a mother. The revolving door of visitors made it that, on top of learning how to be a mom, I also had to entertain — my manners preventing me from saying no to anyone wanting to visit.

I never told anyone about what I was feeling. I never told anyone that it felt like I was a spectator in my own body, instead of being an active participant. I knew I was awake and functioning, but I felt disconnected from my body — as if my body was ethereal. I was watching my feet take me places, and my hands perform tasks, without really feeling in control of them. I seemed to exist in a fog — not really aware of what was happening around me. I was only able to focus on the pinpoint item that was at the front of my mind — my son and his basic needs. I was not able to cope with anything else — not making meals, not doing housework, many days not even getting dressed. I spent countless hours in pajamas or sweatpants.

There were moments where I tried to talk to other mothers — the few that I knew. I didn't have a large network of 'mom friends' at that time and wasn't terribly close to anyone that had small children. I was met with a smile, and a small laugh as they reminisced about how tough it is to have a small baby and how I'd *'figure it out'*. *"We've all been through it,"* they'd say, *"you'll be fine."*

It felt like a pat on the head and a dismissal. The few other mothers around me were all quite a bit older, and all expressed only positive experiences with their postpartum periods. Feeling that my struggles were not understood, and not validated, I quickly stopped trying to talk to others about my struggles. This added to my confusion — *why couldn't I find one person that would simply listen, rather than try to tell me how much more difficult it could be?* "Was I really such a horrible mother that there was no one out there that understood what I was going through?" I said to myself. These types of responses only served to reinforce that others did not struggle as I was — and that if I didn't *'figure it out'* everyone would realize that I wasn't capable of caring for my son, and he would be taken away from me.

There was one person that I wished had still been in my life just after Eddie was born. One person that I felt confident would have at least been able to empathize with how hard being a new mom truly was.

Just prior to marrying Ed, I had become very nervous about trying to become pregnant. I knew, in the months leading up to our wedding, that we had always talked about having children right away. Now that the reality of this was approaching, I was scared. I had dozens of questions. *Were we ready? How would we provide for our kids? Were we responsible enough?*

That all changed one day when I was watching Ed playing ball hockey with his team. My brother and his then-girlfriend, Janelle, came to watch as well, and Janelle brought her son, Ty.

I had a great deal of respect for Janelle. She was a pretty young thing, a few years younger than me — at most, she would have been 22. She lived on her own with her son, worked hard, and Ty was a very polite little boy. He would have been about five years old at the time.

I remember sitting at that game, and watching Ty playing quietly. He was a small boy, crouched down in the stones, playing with his small cars. Dirt smudged on his face, and a happy smile. I watched Janelle as she watched over him, ensuring that he didn't go too far away, and behaved appropriately. Janelle would have been about seventeen when she'd had Ty. I thought about the decisions she'd probably struggled with, and how scared she must have been when pregnant. I was in absolute awe of the incredible job she was doing with her son.

It was like a bolt of lightning struck me at that moment. I thought, *well, hell, if she could do it as a teenager, I can CERTAINLY do it now!!*

Unfortunately, by the time Eddie was born, Janelle was no longer dating my brother. She was not a resource I could call for advice. I felt completely alone. I wished desperately for someone I could talk to that might be able to understand what I was going through.

CHAPTER 10

The first three weeks of Eddie's life, Ed was home with us. It was wonderful! In our whole relationship, Ed and I had never had that much time together, and two sets of hands are better than one when taking care of a newborn! We settled into a routine with Eddie, and as the days went by, I began to be able to manage the anxiety. It still grew every day, and peaked in the evenings, but by the beginning of the second week at home, I was no longer needing to go to my parents to calm down. I was gaining some control, and the hold my black hole had on me was dissipating just a bit.

However, at the end of those three weeks, when Ed went back to work, I was again faced with change, and this time, I was on my own.

At the time, Ed was still working twelve-hour shifts, both days and nights. Ed's schedule was routine, but when he was in a working block, it was difficult to manage with Eddie on my own, especially when Ed was working nights, and I would have to keep Eddie quiet through the day. Being all alone with Eddie sent me spiralling back out of control. The anxiety reared its ugly head, and the feeling of incompetence was paralyzing. It felt like I was back at the hospital, all alone with Eddie, the first evening he was in my hospital room — I was scared of hurting him in some way.

During these times, I spent a lot of my days at my parents' house. The times that I was home alone all day were the worst. My days were spent in a fog, my only real goal was for Eddie to eat and then sleep as much as possible — if he was sleeping, he was happy. If he was sleeping, he was safe. If he was sleeping, I wouldn't have to do anything for him and I wouldn't feel like I'd done something wrong. After the initial struggle to learn how to breastfeed, that task had become something that was very easy for Eddie and me.

When Ed was working day shifts, which ended at 7:00 p.m., I would be at my absolute wits end by the time he arrived home. I had spent the previous twelve hours being at the beck and call of a baby — feeling unable to do anything more than take care of his basic needs. By 7:15 p.m., I would be calling Ed, just to make sure he had left the office and would not be late, as I couldn't stand another moment by myself. He would arrive home, and I would thrust Eddie into his arms, grateful for another person to be there to help. I had not made dinner, as that would have required some form of planning and actually going to a store, with a baby, and buying food to cook. That was simply too much for me to accomplish.

My anxiety was still that electrical current — constantly simmering under the surface. Anything that was out of routine was enough to cause me to explode. I would explode in anger — lashing out at whoever was closest to me. That was usually Ed. Bless him for his infinite patience.

I held a great deal of resentment toward my husband in the first few months of our son's life. While, of course, his life had changed too, at the time it seemed like he really benefited from experiencing the 'good' parts of being a parent and I had to deal with the 'reality' of being a parent. Ed was still able to go out with his friends when he wanted to. It seemed that I was having to make all of the sacrifices. It never occurred to me that had I been honest, and told Ed what I was going through, he would have moved heaven and earth to support me. He would have done anything possible to get me the help I needed.

One of the challenges I found the most difficult was actually where we were living. When Eddie was born, we were living in Virgil, a town in the heart of Niagara on the Lake. When we bought the house, we thought it was perfect, being close to both of our parents and all of our friends. The house we bought was a 45-year-old bungalow that backed onto a peach orchard. It was peaceful, quiet, and a wonderful location to start a family. We could have been happy there for many years. Virgil was a small town, but it did have a couple restaurants, a grocery store, two schools, and several other establishments that made it attractive for a young family.

Ed and I both worked in Niagara Falls, a twenty-minute drive from home. Prior to having children I found this drive a nice way to decompress after work. However, once Eddie came, Virgil felt like it was a million miles away from everything. Other than grocery shopping, EVERYTHING we did was in Niagara Falls — pharmacists, doctors, the OEYC, friends, etc. The twenty-minute drive quickly became a struggle when Eddie was breastfeeding so often, as it really meant a twenty-minute drive both ways. With Eddie feeding every two to three hours, and forty minutes of driving to plan around tasks, the drive added an additional level of anxiety that I simply could not cope with. Unable to objectively look at the problem and begin to breastfeed outside of my home, or introduce a bottle, I simply stopped going out if it wasn't something absolutely critical. I quickly became reclusive and withdrawn. The only time people would see me was if they came to me — and everyone assumed that I was just like any other first-time mom, adjusting slowly. They probably assumed they had caught me on a bad day, and that the dishes in the sink or the laundry on the floor was something out of the ordinary — it was certainly a far cry from the way I took care of my house prior to having Eddie. Back then, the house had been neat as a pin, everything in its place — extremely organized. The rare time I did see others I was never pressed for information, and my rhetorical *"I'm fine, how are you?,"* was enough to suffice for those that asked how I was doing so long as it was presented with a smile.

My life in Niagara prior to having children had been driven by the need to have job security, financial stability, and the dream of becoming a mother. I had worked, and worked, and worked. I would never turn down a shift at the hospital. I was proud of how goal oriented I was, and I was proud of the respect I had earned at the hospital. Without realizing it, though, I had established only a very few good friendships outside of work. I had left Niagara for five years when I was in university, and the friends that I had before leaving were gone. Friendships I had established as an adult had mostly evolved from working relationships.

After Eddie was born, I realized just how work-oriented those friendships were. I was no longer a part of the crew that would hang out after shift, or around the bonfire. I was a mom, and that distanced me from all the young nurses. They simply couldn't understand my life, and I had no desire to go to a club or bar with them, to return home to my baby after. In addition to this, I was living in Virgil — and none of my work friends were. Virgil seemed to be too far for anyone to drive to visit me. While they were still individuals that

I cared for, we were simply living drastically different lives. This caused me to feel very isolated. While I had always had a great quantity of friendships, I was realizing that perhaps they were friendships of convenience, instead of the high-quality friendships I had thought they were.

One of the only good things that I could see at that time about living in Virgil was that our best friends lived right around the corner — Brent and Jana, who were also married.

Jana was among those that had visited me at the hospital, and was a major source of support, but we weren't able to see each other often as Jana worked shifts. Brent worked full time and had a second job. Neither of them had a lot of time for visiting, let alone visiting a couple with a baby.

Unbeknownst to me and Ed, Brent and Jana were having trouble of their own. They split up about a month after Eddie was born, and I was devastated. Brent had been a high school friend of mine and Ed. Ed had been Brent's bestman, and I considered Brent to be a sort of quasi-big brother. We had been through a lot together.

I'll never forget the phone call. Jana was calling to see if she could speak with Ed, her voice cracking as she spoke. That was odd — *why did she want to talk to Ed?* I told her he was home but had just gotten off of working midnights and was sleeping. She didn't cry, she was so incredibly strong. She simply told me that their marriage was over, and that she wanted Ed to reach out to Brent.

I flew into a panic. I ran to our bedroom — it had been Ed's last midnight shift and he was coming onto a few days. I woke him up abruptly, yelling that he had to call Brent. Figure this out. Fix this somehow. I could not lose Jana too. I felt I had already been isolated from friends; Jana was the last one that I felt truly connected to.

Jana was my best friend — and she was hurting. I didn't have the first clue what to do for her. While I was the first to become a mother, Jana was the first to go through divorce. I should have been going to her, reaching out, helping her. I should have been offering a shoulder to cry on or helping her move out. But I was paralyzed — I was chained to my son, in my own house.

To that point, I had never been separated from Eddie, and the thought of leaving him at home with Ed in that first moment never occurred to me.

I should have seen this as a major sign that I was in real trouble. That there was really something wrong with me, and I needed help. Not three months earlier, I had lost my grandmother, and feared for my grandfather's future. At that time, I had done whatever I felt needed to be done and made sure he'd known that I was there. Now, my best friend had lost her husband, and I simply couldn't think clearly enough to find a way to be there for her. To support her. To focus on someone other than Eddie for a moment.

I couldn't help her, when I could barely help myself. I simply did not have the energy at that time to really support her. I needed help myself and had no energy for anyone else except, Eddie. Selfishly, while I was heartbroken for my friend, mourning for the future she had envisioned, for the chaos her life suddenly was, I also mourned for me. Until Jana was back on her feet, I would be losing a major source of support. She would be moving away — back to live with her parents. While it was not far away, it was much further than where she was now, just around the corner and it felt like a world between us. When Jana moved away, I felt truly alone.

CHAPTER 11

When Eddie was nearing his one-month birthday, we reached out to Mary and Jack, the couple we had run into at the OEYC. Like us, they were adjusting to life at home with a newborn. They were having their own new parenting challenges and, like us, didn't have any friends that had young children. Mary and Jack were a year or two older than me and Ed. We became fast friends.

We were invited to their house for a lunch date. The idea was that this timing would work well for the boys feeding schedules. It was a bright, sunny, hot, July day. They lived in the South end of Niagara Falls — about a twenty-five-minute-drive from where we lived, and in a new subdivision. It was the first time since Eddie's birth that I took the time to shower, put on makeup, do my hair, and dress in shorts and a pretty tank top, I looked like I had it all together.

We were supposed to be there for about two hours.

We ended up being there for four hours. We had so much in common. Jack and I had both attended the University of Western Ontario, in London, at the same time, and both in health care with different majors. Mary's parents lived in St. Davids, right down the road from where I had grown up, and her grandparents went to my parents' church. Both couples were high school sweethearts. But more importantly, both of our sons had been in the NICU the first two nights of their lives. Evan had been born two hours earlier than Eddie, and we had been discharged on the same day.

When we left their house that day, my heart was light for the first time in a month. For a moment, I was happy — for the first time I felt that I wasn't alone in my struggles. There was someone in the world that could understand my day-to-day challenges, and she was comfortable being open and honest with me. It was so wonderful to be debating the pros and cons of different parenting paths with someone who had no more experience with a baby than me!!

It was the beginning of a great friendship.

Mary and I spent a great deal of time together that first summer. She was a bohemian sort of girl — very soft spoken, kind and wearing long, flowy, sundresses. Like me, she had always wanted to be a mother and was reading all kinds of books on how to be a better parent. When we met, Evan was having trouble sleeping, and she was implementing a method of sleep training that she had read about. I was in awe of her — she seemed to have infinite patience. She walked with a grace that reminded me of Princess Aurora in Sleeping Beauty — dancing on a cloud. She even looked like Princess Aurora — with gorgeous dark blonde hair. A far cry from the way I felt — still 40 lbs. heavier than my pre-pregnancy weight, perpetually in sweatpants, with my hair in a ponytail. Nothing seemed to rattle her.

As Jack and Ed had gone back to work, and it was now the hottest point of the summer, Mary and I got together frequently at each other's houses. We would drink tea and chat about whatever was new that Eddie or Evan was doing. Each day was a discovery, and we were able to share that. That summer was a scorcher, and we were cooped up inside due to the extreme heat — there was no way a baby could be taken for a walk later than the early morning hours. At home in Virgil the road we lived on at the time did not have any sidewalks, and vehicles constantly sped down it. The thought of taking Eddie for a walk by myself down our road was terrifying, and the thought of driving somewhere to take him for a walk was too taxing. I was anchored to my couch.

The only reprieve I had was visiting with Mary. However, even with Mary, I did not delve too much into how I was struggling personally. Our discussions were focused on the boys — never ourselves. Although I knew that I was feeling extremely anxious, I did not want to admit my own weaknesses. Mary appeared to have everything together, or at least much more than I did. The times that I was with Mary, I was almost able to ignore the anxiety and feel calm. Almost. To be with someone who understood what I was going through — it was such a wonderful feeling.

Befriending Mary did not help with my anxiety at home. The evenings continued to be hard and, other than at Mary's, I was uncomfortable breastfeeding outside of my house. My days were driven only to achieve the goal to make sure Eddie was fed, clothed, and clean. Above and beyond that, there was nothing. I was a machine, with that one sole purpose spurning me on. I was doing very well at my task — Eddie was growing like a weed, and was generally a very happy baby — but I could do absolutely no more in my life.

There were days when the only reason I got out of bed was because Eddie was crying. There were dirty dishes in the sink, and expired food in the fridge. The laundry would lay in heaps throughout the house — a pile in front of the washing machine that needed to be washed, a basket of clean clothes that needed to be folded, a laundry hamper overflowing with dirty clothes. Socially, my relationships suffered. Friendships became fragile with people who hadn't understood my want to be a young mother, and were then lost, when I didn't feel capable of going out to visit. Everywhere I turned, there seemed to be women who had only positive postpartum experiences — not one person seemed to understand my struggles. I was constantly hearing phrases from people that were supposed to minimize what I was going through:

"Having one child is easy. Just wait until you have TWO!"

"Oh, it was so hard when I had my babies because there were no disposable diapers and I had to hand wash every cloth diaper!"

"My husband was working all the time and I'd be home with all three kids all by myself."

Or, the worst one,

"Thank goodness it wasn't twins!"

While these people were trying to empathize with me and make me feel understood, the result was actually the opposite — causing me to feel that, if I was struggling with just one child, I would never be able to have more children. My future as a mother was in jeopardy in multiple ways. If I couldn't really care for one child, how could I have another? If someone discovered that I couldn't really care for one child, would they take him away? Many days my mind would be working in overdrive — creating future narratives that were horrifying. Those awful thoughts would become nightmares, such as Eddie being harmed, Eddie being taken from me, or Eddie hating me when he grew up; which would prevent me from sleeping.

I fell victim of a recurring nightmare of Eddie being harmed in a variety of ways. Night after night, for weeks. He'd be hit by a car, fall off a balcony, kidnapped — injured in some way. The one constant through all of my nightmares was being inches away from him, and unable to stop him from being injured. Watching the car coming, as Eddie ran into the road. Watching as the railing disappeared from the side of the balcony, with Eddie leaning on it. Watching as he was picked up and put into a vehicle that sped away from me. Always his eyes were looking at me — trusting me to protect him. In his eyes was absolute confidence that no harm would come to him as long as I was there. In my nightmare, I was never able to stop him from being harmed. I would wake up, pulse racing, hair standing up on my arms. I would be gasping for breath, and my face would be wet from my tears. Night after night. Many nights I would slip out of bed, as quietly as possible to ensure I didn't wake up Ed, tiptoe to Eddie's crib side and look down — just to be sure that he was still there, and still breathing. The nightmares were always worse when Ed was working nights, and not home, as if my unconscious mind was still telling me that the greatest risk to my son's life was myself.

There were many different versions of nightmares that involved Eddie's death. However, the worst nightmare did not involve Eddie dying. The worst nightmare hit closer to my real fear.

In this nightmare, which occurred repeatedly and was always the same, Eddie and I were at home alone:

It was a bright, sunny, summer day. We were in the living room, which had a large bay window looking out to the street. I was holding Eddie in my arms.

Suddenly, the driveway and street were full of police cars and there were officers all over my front yard — guns drawn. It looked like the scene out of a movie depicting a hostage situation. Police car doors open, officers with their arms around the doors, ready to shoot if necessary.

One officer had a megaphone, *"Come out with your arms up. Leave the baby in the bassinet. Make any attempt to run and we will shoot!"*

They had finally come for me. Someone had tipped them off. They knew that I was the greatest risk to my son's life. My heart racing, tears streaming from my eyes, I looked down and found the bassinet beside me. I looked at my son, staring at me with trust in his eyes, and placed a kiss on his forehead. I lowered him into the bassinet, and I moved to the front door. Opening the door, the bright light was blinding at first.

And then I would wake up. Dripping in sweat, bed sheets twisted around my legs, my face wet with tears. For the first few minutes after my nightmares, I would lay in bed, eyes tightly shut, focusing on my breathing. Trying to slow my heart rate. Trying to stop my hands from shaking. Trying to dispel the fear from my heart.

The nightmares only added to my exhaustion. When Ed was not home during the day, I tried to ensure Eddie slept as much as possible because then, I didn't actually have to do anything with him. There were days when I only got dressed just before Ed came home, so that he wouldn't know how bad it really was.

––––––––––

Having a June baby poses a unique problem.

June is typically the end of programs — school is ending, and in conjunction with that, the main programs being offered through the OEYC were ending. Sessions of any real length were not being offered until September. Through the latter part of June, all of July, and all of August, there were random sessions being offered but they felt disjointed — there was no consistency with the people attending or the times the programs were offered. That prevented any further relationships with other new moms from being established when I was there.

The first session we tried was a baby massage class. The sessions offered were all meant to teach the parent something about parenting, but also to socialize the baby and the parent.

During one trip to baby massage, the school had something going on — it was late June, so likely a graduation ceremony. The parking lot was full, and I had to park on one of the side streets, and carry Eddie in his carseat to the centre. This inconvenience put me in a wicked mood — I'm sure my frustration was palpable at the centre, but it exploded when I got home. Ed couldn't understand why I was so upset about a minor inconvenience and I screamed, *"I don't have to explain this to you — you just need to agree!"* I was becoming more and more unreasonable as the days progressed. It was the last time I would venture to the centre alone, for several months.

Had Eddie been a July baby, or an August baby, the time between birth and the real beginning of structured programs would have been minimal — enough time to adjust to having a baby at home and be ready to venture into the world. However, Eddie was born at the beginning of June, and that left three solid months, of no real programs being offered. The resources that I was able to take part in come September really would have been very beneficial to me when Eddie was first born. The only resource that was available to me was Eddie's pediatrician, but he focused on Eddie — not on me. As Eddie's delivery had been, from a medical point of view, uneventful for me, there was no follow up appointment suggested with either my OB-GYN or my family doctor. While I was meeting with Eddie's pediatrician regularly, the conversation was centered on how Eddie was doing — I was never asked how I was doing. I never thought to ask about myself, my focus in those appointments was on my son. There was no medical professional that pointedly asked how I was handling being a new mom.

By late August, Mary and I had begun looking at the programs that September would bring at the OEYC together. She had found a program called, 'Baby Talk'. Baby Talk was a weekly meeting for new parents. The opportunity to get together in an organized, safe environment and discuss the trials and tribulations of parenthood. The idea was that we could build friendships and support each other, and a consultant was there to facilitate the session and answer any technical questions we may have. Baby Talk was set to begin the first week of September. Both Mary and I signed up.

Despite signing up for the class, I was very concerned about the commitment. It was held in the early afternoon — right during Eddie's naptime. How was I going to adjust his schedule to accommodate the class time? Particularly, as it was held in Niagara Falls — which added the terrifying twenty-minute drive (TWO WAYS!), and the drive had to be considered in the execution of this task. Also, *how was I going to feed Eddie during the class?* The class was two hours long, he would certainly get hungry during that time! He was still only breastfeeding, and I wasn't comfortable with that in public. *What if he had a poop explosion in his diaper and needed to have a full outfit change? What if he started crying during class, and I couldn't soothe him?* My mind was going a mile a minute with possible problems that might occur.

In the days leading up to the first class, I thought up at least half a dozen perfectly legitimate excuses that would get me out of having to attend the class. I went so far as to call the OEYC to cancel, only to hang up when the phone was answered. Never did it occur to me that the whole point of this program was to provide an environment that was welcoming, supportive, and comfortable.

As much as I knew that I was struggling as a new mother, I did not realize that my experience was vastly different from what most other new moms' experience. I had been programmed to believe what others had told me — that I would *'figure it out eventually.'* I didn't realize that I needed outside help. I was operating under the assumption that I would just grow out of this, that it would pass in time. I didn't realize not only that I was struggling more than most, but also that there were resources that I could have contacted to receive the help and support that I needed. I thought I had to figure everything out on my own, and that was incredibly isolating. I never stopped to think that the Baby Talk program may benefit me in some way. Baby Talk was simply a program that Mary wanted to do, and I had agreed to join her.

As the day of the first session grew closer, I reasoned that I had given Mary my word that I would be there, and I would *not* fail my friend. I would be there. Come hell or high water, I would make it happen.

By early September, I had begun introducing a bottle to Eddie. Even though, when Eddie was first born, it seemed to be a popular belief that breastfeeding exclusively is best for newborn babies, many people were still shocked that Eddie was unable to feed from a bottle. They marveled at the fact that Eddie had been solely breastfed — and that it meant he was unable to be away from me for long periods of time. I was so incredibly confused, frustrated, and again I felt I was not doing something 'right' with my son. My fears of someone finding out I was incapable of raising him caused me to take a comment from anyone and extrapolate from that only the negative. I simply wasn't mentally strong enough to let comments slide off my back — everything was taken to heart. Although I'm sure no one was intending to 'shame' me, with my dark state of mind, it was easy to assume that questions about my mothering decisions indicated that I was doing something 'wrong.'

My attempts at bottle feeding were not going well. Eddie had been conditioned to only nurse directly from my breast. We were spending oodles of money on different bottles and nipples trying to find one that he would accept. Additionally, I was trying to adapt to a breast pump. Breastfeeding, while frustrating and painful in the very beginning, had become something that was easy for me. Pumping should have been easy, or so I thought. I was severely mistaken, and I was struggling with the pump.

Every evening, I would attempt to pump enough for a bottle for Eddie. To my astonishment, I could pump for an hour and not have a drop of milk appear. I couldn't understand what I was doing wrong — and pumping exacerbated my feelings of stress and inadequacy. I would produce absolutely nothing. However, when Eddie was hungry, I would produce more than enough for him.

Late one night, I sat on our couch trying to pump. Ed was in the armchair beside me watching a movie. I had been pumping for almost an hour and had no more than a couple of ounces. This had been a nightly ritual for a couple of weeks, and I was beyond frustrated. I didn't realize that I was crying until Ed moved to be beside me, rubbing my back.

"Jess, there has to be an easier way — every night you sit there pumping, and it's just not working," he said. *"Let's try a type of formula for him, it'll be OK."*

I had fought for so long to try and provide only breastmilk for my son, but hearing Ed say he was supportive of trying formula, was a wonderful stress relief.

We made the decision to try formula — *but what kind?* As with the bottles and nipples, we spent oodles of money on different formulas — and Eddie continued to absolutely refuse to take a bottle. There was no possible way that I could attend the Baby Talk classes and not be expected to feed him at some point — a realization that increased my anxiety. I was still not comfortable breastfeeding in front of people — not even other mothers. It was enough to cause me to regret having signed up for the class. It was only because Mary was going that I didn't back out — I would not let my friend down.

CHAPTER 12

The first day of Baby Talk came, and I was a tightly wound bag of nerves. I had spent the last three months nestled in my home. Joining this group meant I had to get up, feed the baby, take a shower, make myself presentable, feed the baby again, feed myself (hopefully twice — breakfast and lunch!), and pack him in the car before journeying to Niagara Falls for the class.

The morning had gone fairly smoothly, which my nerves appreciated very much. I had been so nervous the night before that I hadn't slept well, and I was anxious to get to the group, find Mary, and take a seat. I showed up at the OEYC and entered the main room to find a half circle of moms each in a chair, with a baby on her lap. There were about five at that time, but Mary was not one of them.

Four more women and their babies arrived in the next few minutes and still Mary wasn't among them.

The instructor announced that she was just going to finish up something quickly, and then we would start. I was alarmed. I lifted Eddie onto my hip and chased after the instructor:

Hesitating, I said, *"I'm so sorry, but my girlfriend hasn't shown up yet. I'm sure she's on her way, can we just wait a couple more minutes?"*

"What is your friend's name?" The instructor replied.

"Mary," I said.

The instructor sighed and shook her head. I quickly discovered Mary had called the instructor that morning to state that she wouldn't be coming for the session, *at all*. Something had happened and she had backed out of the class entirely, without relaying this to me.

I was so confused. As much as cell phones and texting were around at this time, texting was a very new thing and not something that I used — ever. We still had a landline at home and people only called my cellphone if there was an absolute emergency. *Why had she not called me??* My disappointment was intense and as I walked back to my seat, with Eddie still on my hip, I contemplated picking up my things and leaving the class.

I felt abandoned. I had entered a room full of strangers, feeling anxious about the hungry baby that I knew my son would soon become, totally out of my element, and now I was all on my own. I could not see how this was going to help me. The bundle of nerves that had been in my stomach became a live wire. *How was I going to get through this class by myself?* There was no one there that would understand what I was going through. I felt a lump in my throat develop, and I willed tears not to leave my eyes as they were threatening to.

I quickly decided that leaving the class at that point would have caused more of a scene than I was willing to make. I sat Eddie on my lap, and took a deep breath as the session began.

Introductions were made and I discovered that, of the children in attendance, Eddie was the third oldest — only trumped by a little girl that was born the last week of May, and a boy born two days before him. The moms participating were all roughly my age — most a bit older, a couple a bit younger, but all of us were first time parents. It levelled the playing field, and allowed us all to feel that we were among friends.

The instructions for the program were simple: Each session would have a theme, which was really just a conversation starter. The sessions were confidential, and we were encouraged to be open and honest. For the first time, I was in the presence of others that were willing to admit that they were struggling — just like I was. For the first time, I was surrounded by people that were really able to level with me — to state that *'you'll figure it out'* was one of the absolute worst things to hear — because it indicated that there was no one in the world that could actually help. I was surrounded by people that were struggling at being a new parent, just like I was — in different ways, with different aspects, but we were all struggling with *something*. For

80

the first time, I realized that maybe I wasn't a horrible mother, and maybe I wasn't doing a terrible job. It was a refreshing experience. As nervous as I had been, I was quickly put at ease and comfortable with these women. For the first time, the anxiety I had been living with, and the fears of myself being the greatest risk to Eddie's life, began to diminish just slightly.

Knowing that Eddie would be hungry at some point during the program, I had brought a bottle of formula, in an attempt to avoid the dreaded breastfeeding in public that I was never comfortable with. But Eddie absolutely would not take the bottle, no matter how hard I tried, and I eventually gave up. Frustrated, I pulled out a blanket to provide some privacy and tried to hide the angry tears that again were threatening to stream down my face.

I looked up and realized that the others were all looking at me. My heart sank. My tears spilled. My worst fear was about to be realized — these women would see what I was desperately trying to hide. They would see that I was incapable of managing my son. Instead of judgement though, I saw understanding on their faces. The consultant walked to me, and she rubbed my arm — reassuring me that I was in a safe space. The conversation pivoted to the struggles of bottle versus breast feeding. I realized that others were tackling the same issue — either at that time, or in the recent past. We discussed various bottle options, and the different nipple options, as well I learned about certain brands of nipples that were more realistic in the look and feel. I was even shown the exact style that the participant had success with, so I would be sure to buy the right one. I also learned about various options for formula — discovering that powdered formula may be gentler on my sons' stomach than the canned liquid and may smell more like my breastmilk. For the first time, since becoming a mother, I felt that I was understood.

The change in my demeanor was palpable. Ed returned home from work to a happy wife, chatting about the session — the people, the discussion, the ideas that had been offered to assist with Eddie's bottle feeding. We immediately went to Walmart and purchased the formula, bottle, and nipples that had been suggested.

The positivity was fleeting, though, and the suggestions were not a miracle-cure for Eddie's aversion to bottle feeding. The next day was back to square one, with me back in sweatpants, no makeup, and the knot in my stomach had returned. But the next session of Baby Talk was only six days away, and I had that to look forward to. It was nice to look forward to something.

Upon my arrival home after Baby Talk, I had reached out to Mary via telephone. She apologized for not having called me. She explained that Baby Talk was right at Evan's naptime, and she just didn't feel that she could manage to bring him to the session because of that.

I was shocked. I hadn't realized that Mary was having the same concerns as I had been having — that Baby Talk would interrupt naptime. For the first time, I wondered if Mary was struggling just like me. I felt horrible for not seeing this, and I realized I'd had a picture in my head of Mary as the 'perfect' mom — having everything together all the time. To me, Mary had been living her life as a bright light — having infinite patience for Evan, never appearing rattled or frustrated. Conversely, I also had a picture in my head of myself as the 'horrible' mom — my life seeming to be one continuous, endless mess of confusion. Compared to Mary, I felt heavy and dark. I began to realize that neither picture was accurate. I told her all about what Baby Talk had been like. She was upset that she'd missed it and was going to call and see if there were still spots available.

Baby Talk was a turning point in my struggle. The effort I had to put in, to prepare both myself and Eddie, and socializing with other new moms, gave me something to look forward to every week. It was a safe zone for me — where I could ask questions that I didn't feel comfortable asking elsewhere. I was also given the opportunity to hear other mom's questions — about things that I hadn't considered or hadn't come up against yet. It was an environment that was one hundred percent positive, supportive, respectful, open, honest, and caring. It was also a commitment of only once per week — which was manageable for me. I did not feel overwhelmed, and actually looked forward to each session.

Baby Talk would also turn out to be an opportunity provider, for another mom and tot program.

At the end of the third Baby Talk session, the third week of Septemb
and a couple of the other moms were asked to stay behind for a few mint
All of our babies had been born between the end of May, and the end of Ju

"There is a program called Roots of Empathy through the local school boai
we were told. *"This program looks for moms that would be willing to he*
their child attend a Grade One classroom in a local school once a mom
beginning in October. It is an anti-bullying program. The theory is that,
the students see your child grow, they develop a protective nature with th
baby, and that transfers to their treatment of all people. The program look
specifically for babies born between the middle of May and the end of June
as those babies will be reaching milestones that are easy for the students to see
and understand — rolling, crawling, walking, etc. The baby is the 'teacher' and
is the most important person in the classroom. If you are interested, please call
the program by the end of the week."

I took the phone number, and I drove home. I was interested, but I was
nervous — I was just getting used to being out in public with Eddie by
myself, and that was only at Baby Talk in a highly regulated environment.
Could I manage him in a room full of children? What if he spit up? What if he
had a poop explosion in his diaper? What if he was miserable, or hungry, or
sleeping? My mind was quickly running away with 'what if' scenarios.

That night, Ed and I were again talking about Baby Talk. Timidly, I
mentioned to him about Roots of Empathy.

"That sounds like a great opportunity for both you and Eddie," Ed said, *"Are*
you considering it?"

I paused, thinking about the commitment, and replied, *"Well, yes, I am.*
I'm not sure about it though — what do you think?"

He glanced at me, trying to hide a smile, *"I don't think it hurts to investigate it."*

I thought about that. My heart was telling me to call the program, but my
head was telling me to go slow.

I waited a day or two. By the end of the week, when I was still thinking
about the opportunity, I knew that I had to make the call and at least check

it out. I was nervous about the unknown, but excited about the opportunity — an anti-bullying program that my son happened to be the perfect age for, and I thought, *how could it go wrong?*

After making the initial connection, things went quite quickly. The idea for Roots of Empathy was to meet with the class once a month for one hour from October to June. There was a liaison — Ralph — who would be at every class. He was just an observer to ensure that everything went smoothly. The class teacher, Mrs. Mack, would have a theme for every month that the students would be using to prepare for our visits — and when we arrived, they would have different activities to show us. Things such as "What does Baby Eddie like to eat?" and they would brainstorm, or "Will Baby Eddie be walking the next time we see him?" and they would take a class poll.

Eddie, or Baby Eddie, as he was called by the class — was the star of the show. There was nothing that he could do wrong. The children were not allowed to touch him unless he touched them.

I thought this was a fantastic idea, and after my initial meeting with Ralph, I was very excited to commit to this program. We were assigned to John Marshall School in Niagara Falls. We would begin visiting the class in mid-October.

Upon our arrival at the school the first day, Ralph met us in the parking lot. He went over exactly what to expect, which helped to settle my nerves considerably. Eddie was sleeping in his car carrier as we walked down the hall, and into the classroom.

The class was one of those 'open-concept' classrooms where there are multiple classes in one large room, sectioned off by bookcases and portable chalkboards. There were four different classes in this particular room, and I could see tiny faces looking at Eddie and I from between the bookcases. In the section that we were ushered to there was a carpet on the floor, and fifteen six-year-olds all sitting in a circle.

The children were all watching as I walked over to the semi-circle. They could barely contain their excitement and were squirming around on the carpet craning their necks to see Baby Eddie. As Ralph made introductions, I noticed a bulletin board that had Eddie's picture on it, the one I had provided previously, and words written around it. Words such as 'crying', 'tiny', 'sleeping', and 'diapers'. It seemed they'd been asked to brainstorm what ideas a baby brought to their minds.

One of the more outspoken little boys called over, *"Where is Baby Eddie?"*

I smiled, and glanced at Mrs. Mack. She gestured to the centre of the circle, and I moved to put Eddie, still asleep in his carrier, down on the carpet.

Suddenly, the circle of children became a semi-circle, with all of them scooting their bums over to see Baby Eddie. They had been working so hard for the past week to prepare to welcome us, and they were absolutely beyond excited.

Mrs. Mack sternly told all the children to resume their previous seats, reminded them that they needed to be calm and gentle around Baby Eddie, and grinned at me. She seemed just as excited to meet Baby Eddie as the children were.

All the commotion caused Eddie to wake, and he started fussing. He gave a big stretch and looked around, finding my face in the crowd. He smiled and yawned.

I went to him and took him out of the carrier. He was sitting up with support by this age, and I put him in my lap, so the children could see him, and he could see the children.

Fifteen sets of large, saucer eyes stared at him. The students seemed absolutely in awe of the little baby. As curious as the students seemed about Baby Eddie, he also seemed very curious about them. He was gurgling by this age, and cooing. He looked at the students, and reached out to them, seeming to want to touch them. A collective *'awwwww'* sounded from the students and they laughed at the drool escaping Eddie's mouth.

I learned that many of them were the youngest in their respective families, and they had never seen a baby before. This was a very exciting opportunity for them, and I was proud that it was made possible because of my commitment.

Roots of Empathy and Mrs. Mack's Grade One class became something I looked forward to, once a month. Our presence was exciting for the children, but also for me. To be able to see the way the children's eyes lit up when Eddie came into the room. To hear their astonishment when they saw what was 'new' — rolling over, crawling, and the most spectacular of all, when he started walking. The day before we arrived, the students always took time to brainstorm what they thought would be 'new', like, "would he be sitting, crawling, walking?"

This program also gave me something to look forward to, and a reason to get out of the house. Roots of Empathy helped remind me of the miracle that a baby truly is and see through the eyes of the students how quickly Eddie was growing. If he spit up, my first reaction was to groan and roll my eyes thinking of the added task of having to change him. However, the children would think it was so cute that Baby Eddie had hiccups and they would laugh. They showed me the silver linings.

I realized the full impact of this program one day the following spring — when Eddie had been part of the program for about six months. I was out for lunch with Eddie and my mother, coincidentally at a diner that happened to be close to the school. As my husband and my son are both 'Eds' we had gotten into the habit of calling them "Big Ed" and "Little Ed" or "Baby Eddie." I was sitting in a booth chatting with my mom and said something about 'Baby Eddie' when a woman at the table across the walkway from me suddenly looked over and said *"Oh my goodness!!! Is that Baby Eddie from the Roots of Empathy program??"*

She was a grandmother whose grandson was in the Grade One classroom that Eddie and I visited on a monthly basis. There had been something about the way she'd heard me say *"Baby Eddie"* that had resonated with her. Her grandson was so thrilled about Eddie's visits that he had been giving her monthly updates about what Eddie was doing. I was so proud that my son had made such a positive impact on someone. So proud that I'd had the strength to take part in that program at a time that I had been struggling so severely. Meeting this grandmother had reinforced that I had done something positive for the children and for Eddie, and that made me feel really good.

CHAPTER 13

By the end of September, when Eddie was almost four months old, I had committed to two different programs — both manageable in their expectations, and both programs that I was enjoying. I found that I was getting out of the house regularly — including showering, putting on makeup, dressing in something other than pajamas and sweatpants, and bottlefeeding in public — which we had finally mastered.

I was about to face another major hurdle — leaving Eddie alone with another person for a couple hours.

To this point, since he had graduated out of the NICU, I had not left him for any length of time. Not once. Eddie and I had always been together.

My birthday is at the end of September, and Ed wanted to take me out for dinner just the two of us. I struggled to wrap my head around this, and made a deal with him — an early dinner, and only dinner — straight to the restaurant and straight home. He agreed, and my mother was recruited to watch Eddie for the two hours that we were out of the house.

By this time, we had managed to find a bottle-feeding option that Eddie liked. He was breastfeeding or bottle feeding every four hours on a regular schedule. The ability to give Eddie a bottle was revolutionary — allowing Ed to be able to feed his son made him feel more connected, and knowing that I wasn't chained to Eddie anymore, was very freeing for me. Now, being with Eddie all the time was something I chose — rather than feeling forced to do. He hadn't been introduced to solid food yet, though that was soon to come, and our early dinner allowed me to return home in time for his bath and bed.

While Ed and I were at dinner, all my mother had to do was change his diaper, if necessary, and possibly give him a bottle, if he got hungry early. No matter, I was still a nervous wreck that day, leading up to the dinner. Again, my mind was running away with *'what ifs'* scenarios, as we talked:

I started, *"what if he started crying and my mom couldn't soothe him?"* *"Then he'll cry,"* Ed said.

Again, *"what if he had a poop explosion in his diaper?"* *"Then your mom will change him,"* Ed said.

I finally realized that I wasn't going to convince my husband, or my mother, to change their minds about this. I brought Eddie into the bathroom with me, and started putting my makeup on.

"Don't worry, you'll be okay," I said to Eddie. *"I'll be home sooner than you realize, and Grammy will take good care of you. You might have to have a cold bottle though because I don't think she can work the bottle warmer, and you might have to miss Little Einsteins, even though you love that show, because I'm sure Grammy will want to watch her own show, but it's okay, you'll be okay."* And so will I, I thought. I was nervous, chatting at a rapid pace to steady myself, and Eddie was happily playing with a couple of his toys.

As time was progressing, I was becoming more confident with Eddie. I was beginning to look at the two of us as a team, figuring things out together. He seemed to enjoy me talking to him, and I did so, at every opportunity — explaining whatever it was we were doing to him, which became a reassuring practice for me. He would look at me and smile, coo, or giggle. He had a fantastic belly laugh, which Ed and I both loved to hear. He was such a happy baby — rarely crying or fussing for no reason. If he was upset, it was usually one of three things — he was dirty, he was hungry, or there was some article of clothing making him uncomfortable.

When my mom arrived, Ed and I were ready to go. Eddie had a fresh diaper on, was just fed, and was happy snuggling with my mom in our armchair. Likewise, my mom looked radiant as we walked out the door. She was so proud to be the first person to be trusted watching Eddie.

I was a nervous wreck during the dinner. I tried not to show it, ate quickly, and refused dessert. We had driven to one of our favourite restaurants in a nearby city, and it was two and a half hours before we were home.

Upon our arrival home, it was dark outside. We could see in the front windows. My dad had joined my mom at some point during our dinner, and they were both standing in the front window, my mom holding Eddie, with huge grins on their faces. Eddie looked content, and I knew that my worrying was all for naught. He was fine, my parents were fine, and I had managed, for the first time, to be away from my son. All in all, I felt that it was a success.

As October rolled around, Mary and I continued to look at programs offered through the Ontario Early Years Centre that we could take part in. She hadn't been able to join the Baby Talk group, as there were no spots available, and she could see how I was benefiting from socializing with other moms — she wanted too as well.

We were able to find two programs that we were both interested in. One was a baby swim class, through the local Boys & Girls Club. Once a week, tailored for babies starting at three months — the boys were the perfect age. Ed and I had always intended to teach Eddie how to swim at an early age, since my parents had a pool and lived on the edge of Lake Ontario. There is just so much water in Niagara — we felt it was the responsible thing to do. This swim class was a great idea.

The second program was again through the OEYC, and it was a parenting class — once a week for two hours, for a total of four weeks. It was held in the evenings and Ed and Jack would also be joining us. While Ed and Jack were going to the class grudgingly, Mary and I were very excited about the opportunity to go out as couples — even if it was to a class, and for only a couple hours.

Again, we recruited my parents to watch Eddie so we could attend the class. This time, though, it was more involved than what they had experienced on my birthday. The class was directly in the middle of bedtime. They would need to put Eddie to bed.

In preparation for this, I had Eddie fed and bathed before my parents arrived. I gave them a bottle, with strict instructions that at a certain time they were to feed Eddie the bottle, then put him in the crib. I showed them how to use the baby monitor (Eddie was already rolling, so we weren't using the AngelCare monitor anymore) and gave them the phone number of the school, Jack's phone number, and Mary's phone number, in case they couldn't reach Ed or me, during the class and needed to. My parents understood that this was a nerve-wracking moment for me, though assured me that Eddie would be fine, and I could enjoy myself.

When we arrived at the class, Jack and Mary had already secured us seats at the back of the room, and there were three other couples in attendance. The first half of class was uneventful — mostly introductions of all of the parents, and what we could expect to obtain from the class. There was one ten-minute break during the class, at which point, I told Ed I wanted to call home and check on Eddie. To my surprise Ed was absolutely adamant — he absolutely *refused* to let me call home to check in on Eddie. He assured me that my parents had everything under control.

I was not happy with this, and stewed in my chair for a moment — until Jack broke and let Mary call home to check on Evan. That was enough for me! There was no way I was not going to call home if she was. Ed rolled his eyes and turned his head as I left the classroom to make the phone call.

I stood in the hallway, hearing my Dad laughing as my Mom was changing Eddie's diaper — he'd had a poop explosion (up the back!) but they were loving every minute of it. Eddie was just fine. My mind was put at ease in that two-minute phone call, and I was able to focus on something other than my son for the first time in four months. I was able to focus on what the teacher was saying, and digest nuggets of information that may help in my quest to be a good mom. We were out as adults, with friends, and for the first time in four months I laughed and actually meant it. I was enjoying myself. It felt so *odd*.

It was the beginning of October. Right around Canadian Thanksgiving again. A year before was when I had discovered I was pregnant. For a year, every conscious thought I'd had was about my baby. What I ate, what I drank, how I moved. During my entire pregnancy, naively, I had expected nothing but absolute happiness when my baby was born. Hard work, yes.

Long nights, sure. Missing sleep, of course. But I had expected to be dealing with all of that happily.

Now, for the first time since my son was born, I could honestly say that I was happy. My son was safe, with people I trusted, even though I wasn't there. I was out with friends, and able to truly laugh. There were moments where Eddie wasn't even on my mind. For so long, I had thought of nothing else but ensuring his safety and doing whatever I had to do to make sure that he wouldn't be taken from me.

My son was safe. He was healthy and growing. I was caring for him competently. Not perfectly, certainly, but perhaps competently. I was not an incapable individual that did not deserve to be a mother. I was beginning to realize that I was not the horrible mother that I feared I was.

Returning home after class my son was asleep in his crib, and my parents had spent a couple hours with their precious grandson. For the first time in a long time, I felt a moment of peace. Little by little, between Baby Talk, Roots of Empathy, swim classes, and now the parenting class, I was gaining confidence in my ability to be a mother. Eddie was growing like a weed, meeting all of his milestones, and we had mastered bottle feeding. As I looked down at my son in his crib, I felt for the first time like maybe I was doing a good job, maybe I was a good mother, maybe I really was capable of raising a child.

For the first time since Eddie's birth, my head felt clear. There was no fog, I was in control of my mind, my body, and my emotions. I felt strong, and healthy.

I felt happy. Being out and being social was allowing me to focus on things other than Eddie and myself. I was being forced to regularly get up, get showered, get dressed, and venture out of the house. I didn't realize it, but I was beginning to LIVE again.

CHAPTER 14

As Autumn rolled into Winter, Eddie turned six months old on December 7th. He had begun cutting teeth and we had introduced baby food to him about a month earlier, which he was gobbling up.

Actually, truth be told, Eddie absolutely LOVED food — particularly carrots. He ate them often, and I didn't realize he was eating too many until the tip of his nose turned orange!! I thought he had nice colouring, but his pediatrician giggled at my shocked face when I realized the pediatrician was right — the tip of Eddie's nose was a definite shade of orange! Ed and I laughed about it at home — and it felt so good to be able to giggle at my 'mistake', rather than wanting to cry at my lack of ability. It felt good to look at Eddie and chuckle. For the first time since Eddie had been born, I was able to laugh *at myself*. I was able to look at the problem, see the solution, and implement it. Eddie wasn't too fond of green vegetables, but they were a fact of his life for the better part of a month, in order to fix the colour of his nose.

As Eddie began to eat more and more real food and was successfully holding his own bottles for feedings, I made the decision to wean him off breastfeeding entirely. It was a bittersweet decision, but he had cut several teeth and I was not enjoying being bitten from time to time during feedings. In the beginning, learning to breastfeed was one of the biggest challenges I had, but over time it had become incredibly easy. It had evolved from a task that made me feel trapped, to special moments that only I could have with my son. He was growing, and I was sad to have to say goodbye to this task, although in my heart, I knew he was ready.

One December morning, I settled onto our sofa, with Eddie looking up at me. For the last time, I felt the milk letdown, felt my son calm as his tummy filled. I looked at him and, if there was ever one moment when I fell in love with him, that was it. Suddenly, I was experiencing the emotional connection that had been missing all those months ago in the hospital. I had fallen in love with my son slowly. Unbeknownst to me, I had been bonding with my six-month-old for some time, seeing him in a new way. There was no huge moment of 'Ah-ha!" It was a slow realization that if anything were to ever happen to him, I would be absolutely devastated. A realization that I would do absolutely anything for him. A realization that he was the absolute most important thing in my life, and I loved him dearly. As I cradled my son in my arms after breastfeeding him the last time, I knew without a doubt that he was the best thing that had ever happened to me. It had taken six months, but I was finally confident that I was capable of raising my son, and I was able to face the day's tasks knowing that I was capable of completing whatever they were. I was finally believing in myself.

The crippling anxiety was not gone, though had lessened enough that I was regularly tidying the house, calling friends, and going out to one of the aforementioned programs, two to three times a week. Eddie was sleeping through the night, able to sit up — which meant that he was able to play with toys, and that he could sit in front of toys that had lights and sounds he could create by touching buttons. He was thrilled with this! He would hold his own bottle and wanted to feed himself — always resulting in food all over his highchair, face, and floor. The fact that the mess caused me to laugh, and not cry, was one small victory for me. I was enjoying being a mother, and all the experiences that came with. He was learning to crawl, and enjoyed trying to chase after our cat, Bella.

I reveled in watching my son, realizing that Eddie was SUCH a happy baby. He had a fantastic laugh — a true deep chuckle. He was happy, healthy, and growing. I began to reflect on the last six months and feel that I hadn't made such horrible mistakes after all. He was healthy and happy and growing because of the good care that I was providing. This realization allowed the blackness to begin lifting. It allowed the tightness in my chest to begin loosening. I was beginning to truly breathe again and function at a level that was almost normal.

Then one day, in mid-December, I felt the motivation to cook. I hadn't made a real meal since before Eddie had been born. Breakfast had become something always from a box, and usually, lunch as well. Dinners Ed would take care of, whether that be something in the kitchen or something ordered out. By the evenings, the anxiety had been so intense that I hadn't been able to cook a meal, but had blamed my lack of motivation on being too tired if anyone ever questioned me.

Prior to having Eddie, I was a huge *Food Network* fan. Rachael Ray, Giada de Laurentiis, Ina Garten — I could watch them for hours a day. Although I wasn't a great cook, I thoroughly enjoyed the cooking process. I began watching my favourite shows again. Feeling the motivation to cook, I began watching for a recipe that I might be able to execute. One day, I saw a recipe for pasta with gorgonzola cream sauce. It sounded easy enough, but impressive at the same time. Eddie and I ventured to the grocery store, picked up the required ingredients and got to it! We went the full nine yards — Caesar salad, garlic bread, even a bit of red wine. Eddie sat in his highchair as I cooked, gnawing on croutons or smashing a bit of the sauce.

The look on Ed's face when he walked in, and smelled an actual home-cooked meal, was shocking. He was obviously pleased to see a smile on my face, and I was happy to be feeling motivated and capable of doing more. The meal was decent, but the underlying feeling of accomplishment and being capable of executing a large meal was incredibly rewarding. Now I was not only becoming a social creature again, but I felt motivated to fill the role of wife and mother. Eddie sat in his highchair and attempted to eat pasta noodles for the first time.

After the meal, I sat back snuggling with Eddie as Ed cleaned the kitchen. For the first time in a very long time, I felt proud. I felt happy. Both of my boys were happy. It was a wonderful victory.

Eddie was teaching me that a crucial part of living is simply enjoying the time that I had with loved ones. I didn't always have to be 'doing' something. I didn't always have to have a project I was working on, or a goal that I was working towards. There didn't always have to be a job to do. I had nothing to prove to anyone. I was learning that sometimes the most important times are when you simply stop and breathe and live.

CHAPTER 15

O ver the next few months, there were good days and bad days. Days that I flourished — continuing to cook, attend Roots of Empathy, and swimming lessons. Days that I floundered — having to force myself to take a shower, get dressed, and get out of the house. The difference now was that I was much more mindful of what I had to do to have good days. Not every day began well, though I learned that by leaving my house, I could change the way I was feeling.

Leaving the house was crucial to my mental health. It forced me to have to get dressed, wash my face, perhaps shower, and put on makeup. Even if it was only to go for a walk around town, leaving the house forced me to get out of my pajamas and gave me a feeling that I had accomplished something. My goal was to make each day as good as possible. As my mind continued to lift from the darkness, I began to see what I had gone through the first six months of Eddie's life. My nursing background told me what I needed to know; that I had experienced significant postpartum depression. I still had difficult moments, but the black hole had lost its hold on me, and I could breathe again. I no longer felt stretched, and no longer had a constant knot in my stomach.

As I reflected on Eddie's first six months, I wondered what he would have experienced: *Would a baby feel anxious? Would a baby feel scared? Would there be any long-lasting effects from what I had been feeling that may have affected my son? Had anything I'd done scarred him for life?* I didn't think so — Eddie was such a happy baby. While I was grateful that my struggles had not been worse, and that self-harm or harming my son had never occurred to me, I had to also reflect on what I thought Eddie would have experienced. I vowed that I would never again allow myself to feel so helpless and scared. I was gathering the strength and confidence to advocate for myself in the future, if required. As the months continued, and spring came again, I started looking at my return to work which was scheduled for the end of May.

Ed had received a promotion at work. Instead of twelve-hour shifts, he was now working eight-hour days, Monday to Friday with weekends off. While it was wonderful to have him home earlier every evening, and not have the stress of him working midnights, it complicated my return-to-work plan. I successfully applied for a weekend job at one of the local seniors' homes, to reduce the amount of time that Eddie would need to be at a daycare or with a babysitter.

I was looking forward to being back to work — socializing as a healthcare provider, using my training again, and helping residents and their families. I was also still working on the surgical floor at the hospital — but on an inconsistent basis, and only when they needed help.

In April, as my return to work was looming, Ed and I had begun discussing another baby. We wanted Eddie to have a little brother or sister who was close to his age. Prior to discussing having another child, I knew it was time to sit Ed down and explain what I had been through during the first six months of Eddie's life.

It was a hard conversation. Ed and I had been high school sweethearts. Ed was one of my closest confidantes. We had been together for many years, and he knew me better than anyone. To tell him that I had hidden, so completely, a huge part of my life, was terrifying. I feared that he would be angry. I feared that he would be hurt. I feared that he would not WANT another child, knowing that my deepest concern had been that I would harm my baby.

One night, I sat Ed down, after Eddie had gone to sleep, and told him about my experience. Right from the moment that I felt was the true beginning; when I had the injection of Demerol, to the moment that I felt had started turning things around; when I attended Baby Talk, to the first moment that I truly felt I had control back in my life; and when I was able to cook a large dinner for him. I tried to explain all the main moments that I felt were necessary for him to know without going into explicit detail. The details were something that were very personal, and it would be years before I would really analyze my experience, what I believed the root causes to be, and accept that there was no way for me to have prepared for this time of my life.

Ed admitted that he had known that something was not right, but had chalked it up to my just being a new mother. He hadn't realized the severity of what I had experienced, nor how long I had truly been struggling for. That was difficult for him. He felt he had failed me somehow. Though, I assured him that it was not his fault, that he hadn't done anything to cause what I had gone through. I had gone to great lengths to hide my struggles. I did not go into detail on how bad it actually had been, as I didn't want to make him feel any worse than he already did. However, I did explain what some of the warning signs were — my extreme irritability, struggling to get out of bed and get dressed, my inability to keep the house tidy, and for me, the biggest warning sign was not leaving the house. Ed was incredibly supportive, respecting my request to discuss this with only those I chose to discuss it with, and listening to my fears for any future children.

My struggle with postpartum depression was, at the time, the most confusing personal experience I had ever been through. It was *my* mental health, and my story to share if I chose to.

While I knew I wanted another child, I was worried that the risk of postpartum depression could reoccur. I was also keenly aware that not everyone would understand what I had been through, and that not everyone would be supportive. I feared there would be people that would question my ability as a parent; and judge me based on their personal biases and stereotypes.

At the time I was going through this, there was not a great amount of information in the media about mental health. Society generally failed to understand that mental health was a true health problem. The idea of being asked why I couldn't *'just get over'* or *'figure out'* what caused my postpartum depression was not something I wished to discuss with just anyone. I did not want to answer questions about my struggle, as I was still trying to understand it myself. I feared that, by telling too many people what I had gone through, there may be people I did not completely trust that would know an intensely personal part of my life. The last thing I wanted was anyone watching me closely, or people asking if I was okay. I wanted to be able to ask for help if I needed it, but not have a constant reminder of what I considered to be the hardest time of my life. I was still trying to understand it myself, and I had no desire to discuss it with others. However, it was important for me to reflect upon my experience and the feelings I'd had — in order to try and prevent it from happening again.

As Ed and I discussed having another baby, I was confident that, if I struggled again, I would know where to go and who to ask for help. I would visit my doctor if I felt I was unable to manage with another new baby and seek assistance. I knew that there were resources out there to help if I needed them. With experience comes wisdom. Having experienced postpartum depression once, I knew how it had felt for me, what my triggers were, and most importantly, that it was okay to ask for help if I needed it. It did not mean that I was a bad parent.

My hope for my next pregnancy was that I would experience the moment of instant, parental bliss and overwhelming love for my child that I had always been told would happen immediately after their birth. That moment had been stolen from me with Eddie, and I was willing to do anything to ensure it was not stolen again.

It was easy, with spring air and sunshine, to forget what postpartum depression had felt like. As much as I was certain I knew what to look for, should postpartum depression become my reality after another baby, there was no way to be certain that it would manifest in the same way a second time. It did concern me that I might not recognize it a second time, despite my experience. *What if my postpartum depression came back after a second baby but presented in ways that were different from after Eddie's birth? How could I be sure that it will not happen again?* After a great deal of personal reflection and lengthy discussions with Ed, I realized that there was no way I *could* ensure that this absolutely would not happen again. All I could do was try to be as mindful of my mental state as possible, and to know that Ed was fully supportive and willing to speak up if he saw anything concerning. With that in mind, we decided to roll the dice and try for another baby. However, we also decided to wait until Eddie turned one before trying for another baby. I returned to work the last week of May.

Eddie's first birthday came and went. It wasn't long before I again began feeling like there might be a baby on the way. I had again begun monitoring my monthly cycle but had only just begun. I missed my first period, and as day twenty-eight became day twenty-nine, this time I was much more in tune with my body. The changes were again happening. As with Eddie, this time I was experiencing extreme exhaustion, nausea, and my clothes were already fitting tighter.

I found that with my second pregnancy, I was more relaxed. I'd been through all of this before, and that experience brought a measure of comfort. This time, when taking a pregnancy test, I didn't bother to wait for Ed to go to work and I didn't bother to wait for the morning. I simply bought a pregnancy kit on my way home from work one evening, at the only pharmacy I passed, this time not caring if the clerk wondered about my purchase. I took the test while Ed was giving Eddie his bath five feet from me. We waited together. We looked at the twin lines. Unlike with Eddie, there was no faintness about the second line. There was no mistaking that our next baby was on its way with both lines being clearly present!

Again, I was overjoyed. It had been so easy. It almost took the fun out of it. This time, though I was older and wiser, I was a little scared. Not scared of the responsibility of being a mother, not scared of the pregnancy, but scared of having complications during the birth again, and of having the postpartum depression recur.

This baby was due on February 24th — coincidentally, my mother's birthday. I was happy that this time there was no chance for a heatwave in my ninth month of pregnancy.

They say no two pregnancies are the same, and my two certainly were not. This time there was no overwhelming nausea. I experienced bouts of morning sickness once or twice, but nothing that was unmanageable. The fatigue was greater in the beginning, most likely due to having to chase a toddler who liked to run, not walk. I was working a great deal, but it was much easier working at the nursing home as opposed to the surgical floor. As the RN on duty in the evening, my tasks were mostly medication distribution, patient admission, and scheduling relief staff if someone called in sick for their next shift. The shifts were only eight hours long, and there wasn't a lot of management, doctors, or families to deal with. I got along very well with my coworkers. The heavy lifting was left mostly to the Personal Support Workers, which I was very grateful for this time around.

Eddie was a happy child, and an incredible joy in my life. I thoroughly enjoyed playing Tonka Trucks, dinky toys, and watching Cars the movie with him — on repeat! If the baby was a girl, I hoped that she would be a tomboy with grit — again, as with my first pregnancy, I was hoping for a strong, independent little girl. I envisioned having a daughter who was stronger of character and mind than I had been growing up. Not shy and reserved like I had been as a child.

Again, Ed and I began debating names. Our girl name was still the only one we were ever able to agree on — Camryn Elizabeth. If the baby was another boy though, we were starting from scratch. We'd never considered a second boy name as we had always known what our first son's name would be. To this day, however, I love the name we did agree on. If the baby had been a boy, his name would have been Philip Gregory Friesen. There's still something that rolls off the tongue about that one that is intensely satisfying to me.

This time, we had decided early on that we wanted to find out the sex of the baby when we were able. It had been such a joy to be able to call the baby by his name when I was pregnant the first time and refer to him as 'he' — even before he was born. Again, after the ultrasound, Ed and I visited the OB-GYN together and were thrilled to discover that we were having a girl.

Suddenly, Camryn was born in my mind and my heart. I was so incredibly excited for my daughter, and the opportunity to have a little girl to watch grow up. Just like with Eddie's pregnancy, I would talk to Camryn all the time in my belly. She was already proving to be more challenging than her big brother. I felt her kicking earlier, she caused incredible heartburn, and, as Eddie had, she liked to wedge her feet up under my ribcage. However, she would refuse to allow me to massage them back down. I was learning quickly that she was a force to be reckoned with.

The headphones were brought back out and, just like with Eddie, I played classical music for her. Of course, Ed ensured there was a bit of rock as well. One day, when carrying Eddie to bed, I had him placed directly on my belly. To my astonishment, Camryn gave a firm kick right to her brother's bottom! The look of surprise on Eddie's face was priceless, and I began letting Eddie lay on my belly from time to time — he loved to feel his sister, although I'm not sure he quite understood what was happening.

As the months went on, Eddie graduated from his crib to a big-boy bed. It was really just a mattress that we placed on the floor of our third bedroom. The room was painted deep blue, and was decorated with paraphernalia from the movie 'Cars'. He loved his new room and was happy to hand over the nursery to a new baby. The nursery was kept in its Winnie-the-Pooh theme. The soft greens and yellows were really lovely.

While I was pregnant with Camryn, there seemed to be a baby boom in Niagara, or perhaps it just seemed so because by that time, I was surrounded by women of childbearing years who were having babies. Many of these women were having their second child, but there was one fellow nurse in particular, that was pregnant for the very first time.

One night shift, the two of us were sitting at the nurses' station with an older nurse, discussing our pregnancies and what she should be preparing for. While the other nurse was making comments very similar to what I had heard during my pregnancy with Eddie — "Oh, you'll figure it out", and "Oh, childbirth is such a natural and wonderful experience — you'll forget the pain as soon as they place the baby in your arms," I was very quiet. I wanted to be honest with this girl. She was young, excited to be pregnant — she reminded me very much of myself during my first pregnancy. She was giggling, acutely interested in the advice that was being given, and she turned to me and asked, "any words of wisdom, Jess?"

I sighed and took a deep breath.

"Look," I said, "I'm not going to lie. I really struggled after Eddie was born. His birth was tough. Yes, you forget the pain. I mean, clearly — I chose to become pregnant again! But it is hard being a new parent. You need to find your rhythm and know to utilize *the resources that are available to you. Don't be afraid to ask for help. Take things one day at a time."*

She smiled, and seemed a bit confused. Before she could ask me to explain, a patient bell rang, and she was off to assist the patient.

The older nurse turned and attacked by telling me:

"How could you say that? What were you thinking? She needs to hear that everything will be alright. Yes, parenting is hard but she knows that — she needs people to support her, not scare her!"

My jaw dropped. I hadn't thought of it as scaring the girl. I had only thought that I'd wished someone had been open and honest with me.

I felt like I had been slapped in the face!

'How could I say that?' Was I supposed to lie to that girl? Was I supposed to sugar-coat everything? Better that I simply say nothing.

I was sure that, for some people, the experience of having a new baby is a wondrous, beautiful time. Surely, though, there must be just as many new parents that truly have fleeting moments of regret, and long moments of anxiety in the postpartum period.

Instead of being encouraged to have open, honest, candid conversations, I was told not to share my experience in case it may scare the soon to be parent; which was something I started to notice when I began opening up about my struggles, and it continues to be a problem today: No one wants to talk about it!

I couldn't stop thinking, that if I didn't tactfully, honestly provide advice, the pregnant nurse may feel like I did — lost, scared, and alone. I didn't want her to begin parenthood in the horrible way I did. But I was stunned into silence, and the pregnant nurse never asked me to explain what I'd said.

CHAPTER 16

Eddie had made his appearance to the world twelve days earlier than his due date. So, just in case, we prepared for another early birth. We arranged with my parents that, whatever time labour began, we would first bring Eddie to their house, then carry on to the hospital. We had the diaper bag packed and ready to go by the end of January.

It turned out to be an extraordinarily good thing we prepared early.

Sunday, February 1st, 2009 started like any other day.

Eddie was an early riser and he had taken to coming to my bedside prior to sunrise. I always pulled him into bed with me and Ed — trying to get a few more precious minutes of sleep before starting our day. This time though, when I pulled Eddie into bed at just before 6:00 a.m., I laid back down and felt a twinge through my belly.

"That was odd," I said to Eddie.

Eddie soon fell asleep, and I could hear him and Ed peacefully breathing beside me in the bed.

Ten minutes later — another twinge.

I laid in bed for an hour monitoring the twinges — they weren't strong, but they were extremely regular. Every eight to ten minutes, a twinge. Having never really experienced 'going into labour' with Eddie, due to being induced, I wasn't sure if this was true labour. I decided to err on the side of caution and by 7:00 a.m., I was getting up out of bed, and showering. Eddie was awake again as well, and I ensured he was dressed and fed. At 8:00 a.m., I woke Ed up, and told him what was happening. He showered and we headed over to my parents' house.

I was certain that, if anything, I was experiencing Braxton-Hicks contractions. This couldn't possibly be real labour. It was almost four weeks until Camryn was due. It was Superbowl Sunday, and Jack and Mary were coming over later with Evan for a party.

From my parents' house, I called the hospital, and explained to the charge nurse what I was experiencing. Just to be sure, she encouraged me to go to the hospital — reasoning that at least that way I could be examined. By 9:00 a.m., Ed and I were heading up to the hospital. As we drove to the hospital, I remarked to Ed that it was nice we weren't having to drive through a snowstorm — which had been a concern of mine with a February due date. The sky was a gorgeous blue, with only a few large puffy white clouds in the sky. It was bitterly cold out, but there was no snow on the ground. The drive was an easy one without much traffic. We arrived at the hospital quickly, both of us laughing and placing bets on how long it would take for the nurses to send us home.

That was not to be. While the contractions were not gaining in intensity, they were definitely increasing in frequency. When the nurses examined me, they stated that there was no way I would be going home. My body was already well on its way to being ready to deliver the baby.

Ed and I were absolutely astonished. Phone calls were quickly placed to our parents letting them know that their granddaughter was coming. Ed also placed a phone call to Jack and Mary laughing as he jokingly apologized for our daughter interrupting the Superbowl game.

Camryn's birth is a stark contrast to Eddie's. Due to the complications caused during Eddie's birth, and the first few days of his life, by the Demerol I had received, I was steadfast that I would deliver my second child without any pain relief. I was NOT going to risk getting off on the wrong foot with my second child, as I felt that had been a major factor in my postpartum depression with my first.

This delivery, however, seemed easier. The contractions were gaining in intensity but nothing that was unmanageable. I was the only labouring woman in the department that day. I was so comfortable that Ed and I actually ventured to the family waiting room as it had the only television, and we spent an hour watching *The Comedy Network.*

My OB-GYN, the same one I'd had for Eddie, had been called, but was travelling back to Niagara from Toronto. If the baby was in a rush, I'd have to settle for having the on-call doctor deliver her. Luckily, however, Camryn waited, and my doctor arrived around 4:30 p.m. He performed an examination that caused the labour to kick into high gear.

Cam had one more surprise in store before she was born.

Camryn was born breech — bum first. By the time the nurses realized this, there was no time to elect for a Cesarean section procedure— which is usually the standard procedure in order to ensure the safety of mom and baby. Being four weeks early though, she was a little on the small side at just under 7 lbs. In total I pushed for five minutes, and Camryn was born at 5:14 p.m.

I was totally lucid for the entire labour and delivery, and immediately after her birth she was placed on my chest. We bonded instantly, and the tension I felt was not in the pit of my stomach but in my heart — exploding with love for my child. No complications. No anxiety. I was in control. I was in love. It was such an incredibly different feeling than when Eddie was born. I finally understood what everyone was talking about when they said they absolutely fell in love with their child immediately.

My parents had been hosting a Superbowl party themselves and Eddie was the bell of the ball. My dad and brother had taught him how to put his arms up and yell "Touchdown!" — which he proudly showed off. When they received the call from Ed, stating that their first granddaughter had arrived, they put a trusted friend in charge of the party and left their guests — bringing Eddie to the hospital to meet his new sister.

It's a magical moment when your children meet. Eddie entered the delivery room, and I was holding Camryn. He came up to my left side, and Ed picked him up so that he could look at his sister. His saucer-sized eyes and smile told me that he was as much in love with her as I was.

Ed, Eddie, and my parents stayed until Camryn and I were moved to a postpartum room. It was a brand-new experience. I had my baby in a bassinet beside my hospital bed from the first night. I never even saw the NICU. It was glorious. I felt so proud. I felt in control, there was no fear and there was no anxiety. I knew what to do with my daughter, and how to take care of her. I needed minor assistance to get the hang of breastfeeding again, but quickly settled back into the rhythm of having a newborn.

Cam and I spent two nights at the hospital. This was simply due to the fact that she had been born in the evening, and the nurses suggested that it would be a good idea to spend a second night. I was again in no great rush to leave, and if the nurses thought we should stay, we would stay. We arrived home on Tuesday, February 3rd.

In September of the previous year, I had signed Eddie up for a new music class — called Kindermusik, and with several of the moms and babes that we had known through Baby Talk. By coincidence, Eddie's next session of Kindermusik began the evening of February 3rd. In a show of strength that I would never have dreamt of after Eddie was born, I suggested that we all go to Kindermusik. I'll never forget the look on my friends' faces when I walked in carrying my newborn daughter. Ed sat to the side of the room with Camryn, as I joined Eddie around the circle to sing, play instruments, and dance.

I was strong, confident, and happy. I was in control.

CHAPTER 17

My postpartum depression after Eddie's birth was long, six months, at least. While pregnant with Camryn, I was able to reflect on that time, learn about myself, and what my triggers may have been. My experience allowed me to be able to plan for a potential battle with postpartum depression after Camryn's birth, a battle that was not to be realized.

When Camryn came home there were several things that we did differently, to ensure a smooth transition as possible. I pumped breast milk right from the beginning, so that Ed was always able to give Cam one bottle every day. We agreed that it would be the early night feeding — around 11:00 at night. This way, I was able to get a few hours of solid sleep before waking for her second nightly feeding. Being able to ask for and accept help from those around me that I trusted, was crucial for my mental health. I now realized that I didn't need to do it all by myself, and that others would also appreciate having a hand in helping with the baby. I had family all around me but hadn't felt comfortable asking for help after Eddie was born. That was a stark contrast to the help I asked for, and received, while pregnant with Camryn, and after she was born. I was willing to reach out for help, and my parents were reaching out to ask if they could help — they were happy to be involved.

My sister, in particular, was a great source of support and infinite patience during my pregnancy with Camryn. While she was not privy to my struggles, as I only told my parents and husband, she was happy to be more involved with her niece and nephew. Shortly before Cam was born, my sister and I were together at our parents' house. With my belly being large, and a toddler that I had to keep an eye on, Angie kindly asked if I'd like anything from the kitchen to drink. Grateful, I asked for a glass of water.

She brought me the glass back and I eyed it skeptically.

"What's wrong?", she asked.

I looked up. I knew it was outlandish, I knew that I would never hear the end of it from her, but I simply had to say, *"Can I have a glass of water with no ice? It's too cold on my teeth."*

Her jaw dropped. Her eyes bulged. She took a deep breath and reached for the glass. Muttering, she went back to the kitchen and returned with a fresh glass of water — with no ice.

———————

Ed's birthday is in mid-February and I left my daughter for the very first time that evening, for a couple hours, to celebrate his birthday with dinner at one of our favourite restaurants. My sister and mother were recruited to watch both Eddie and Camryn while we went out. Leaving my two-week-old daughter was an accomplishment that I would not have even dreamed of when Eddie was first born. It also would not have been a possibility as he wasn't bottle-feeding. Camryn being able to drink from a bottle changed the way we were able to raise her in the first few months. There was no rush for us to return home because the baby would be hungry, and I was confident that my children were safe with my mother and sister.

Camryn was a wonderful second child. She slept well, cried only when she was hungry or dirty, and enjoyed simply watching her surroundings. As she grew, she loved watching her big brother running around and he doted on her as any big brother should.

One evening, when Camryn was about three weeks old, I was holding her and watching as Ed gave Eddie a bath. Eddie was playing with his toys, and the bubbles, scooting his bum around the slippery tub. Ed was sitting on the ground beside the tub, laughing. Ed looked up at me, holding his daughter, and down at his son. We both smiled at each other. At that moment, I felt that my family was complete and perfect. It was a moment of perfect happiness.

While life was feeling good, it wasn't without its challenges. One late February day, I had a moment where I felt anxiety setting in. Ed was at work, and I was home alone with the kids. As I looked outside, at the dreary, grey day, I felt my pulse quickening, and my stomach started to knot. I had been feeling unsettled that morning but had no real 'symptoms' I'd been able to pinpoint aside from simply feeling unsettled. I recognized in this moment that I was on my way to a potential anxiety attack. My breathing hitched and I stopped in my tracks. I'd been walking through my living room having just taken Eddie out of his highchair after breakfast. Camryn had already eaten and was napping in her crib. Aside from the dreary weather, there was nothing that I could think of that caused this feeling. Camryn was a wonderful sleeper, and we were all getting a good amount of rest at night. Instead of panicking at the first sign of anxiety, I bundled both kids up into the double stroller we had purchased and took a walk.

It wasn't particularly cold — that winter was shorter, and the mild spring weather was already beginning. Getting out in the fresh air helped, as did the exercise it allowed. I was able to hear birds chirping, and there were buds on the trees to be seen. While the walk helped to calm my nerves, I continued to feel slightly unsettled. So, I again bundled both kids up and drove to my parents' house. I spent the day with my mother and returned home when Ed was there. It was the only time after Cam was born that I had the slightest hint of anxiety. While I wasn't able to determine what caused this feeling, I was proud to be able to recognize it and take measures to mitigate it. At the end of the day, that's all that I could hope for. To know myself and try to identify what my triggers are; and to avoid or minimize those triggers that I could identify to the best of my ability.

One of the most significant triggers, for me, was the inability to leave the house. To feel trapped and unable to leave the house. It was easy for anyone to see that this was not a problem after Cam's birth. I was constantly out with both kids — to Eddie's various activities, shopping, out with friends and family. I was not cooped up in my house, and I was even willing to leave both kids with a trusted friend or family member for an hour or two of me-time. In a strange sort of irony, sometimes that meant going home and having a cup of tea all by myself in my living room or on my back patio.

During my pregnancy with Camryn, the 2008 Financial Crisis was beginning, and around the time of her birth it was hitting its peak. Businesses were closing, and some selling off properties to try and evade bankruptcy.

At that time my father had been the owner/operator of the family business for almost thirty years. It was at this time that the opportunity presented itself to purchase two new properties for the company. Both sites had convenience stores on them, and that was an area of business that he had not ventured into as of yet. He knew that I had wanted opportunities to get out of the house, and he needed help developing the convenience stores. Someone needed to meet with potential suppliers and negotiate contracts. Well, I'd never done that before, but I was happy to learn. It gave me small moments of time away from the kids — and my mother was happy to help watch them and spend time with her grandchildren. Helping my dad allowed me the luxury of having adult conversation, and it had allowed me to feel like I was contributing to the family company. Six weeks after Camryn was born, in stark contrast to what I had been doing when Eddie was six weeks old, I actually found myself leaving my kids for an entire day and venturing to a convention in Toronto. I needed to bring my breast pump with me, and I used it while in the parking lot. I returned home, excited to see my children, and feeling successful in my venture. This feat would have been absolutely impossible after Eddie was born. I had come a long way, and I was very proud of myself.

Unknowingly, by agreeing to assist my father with this, I had taken the first step towards a career change. I never returned to healthcare. I opened those two convenience stores by that July, and by September of the next year had overseen the renovation of two of our existing sites and the opening of convenience stores on them.

I had entered the world of business, and it was a huge learning curve for me. Five years later, in August 2014, I took over as third generation owner/operator of the family company — a moment that has led to many opportunities in my life. One of these being the opportunity to take part in various philanthropic pursuits, which eventually provided me with the opportunity to speak about my journey with postpartum depression. That speech, and the impact it had on women in the audience, was the catalyst that motivated me to write this book. Multiple women came up to me, tears in their eyes, after my speech. Multiple others reached out to me via email. I hadn't realized, when preparing for that speech, the impact it would have on so many others. I knew then that perhaps my struggle could be turned into an opportunity to help others. I would try to take the most negative time of my life and give it a silver lining. As I have grown, and matured, I have taken time to truly reflect on my life and my experiences, and to plan for my future. I want to ensure that, in forty years when I am old and grey, I can look back and know that I made a difference in this world. That's what I want my legacy to be.

I am grateful for my journey with postpartum depression. It showed a young me that I don't have to make it look like I'm perfect all the time. I don't have everything under control, and I still need help from time to time. I am much more open to asking for help now. I now understand that it doesn't mean I am weak, or incapable.

Remember, that goes for you too.

EPILOGUE

I heard my name being announced over the loudspeakers, but it seemed to be muffled in my ears. I could hear my heart beating louder than any voices.

I rose from my seat, and slowly walked to the podium. I willed my hands to stop shaking, before looking out at the thousand eyes staring back at me. I took a deep breath, and from there, I began.

Good morning.

Is everyone awake?

Had your coffee?

I know it's early, but thank you everyone for coming out. I know it means the world to everyone involved to have you all here.

My name is Jessica Friesen and I am current owner/ operator of Gales Gas Bars Limited. Gales is a 52-year-old, Niagara based business and five years ago, I became the third generation to lead the organization. Which means, between my grandfather and my father, a Bob Gale ran the company for 47 years. I've had hundreds of people ask me in my life "Are you Bob Gale's daughter?", as if that was my identity. I'd respond, "Yes! And my name is Jessica". So if I can ask for my first favour of 500 people in Niagara, the next time you see my Dad say, "Are you Jessica's father?" — it's about time the tables were turned.

As I said, I'm the owner/operator of Gales. At Gales, we

are proud to employ almost 100 Niagarans, at our 15 retail locations, our head office, and delivering petroleum products to every municipality in Niagara. We are truly a regional company.

I was asked to speak at today's breakfast because I have had the privilege to commit to being this years' Leadership Sponsor for United Way Niagara's capital campaign. I'm not sure, but I'm going to go out on a limb and say that means that not only does this years' campaign have the youngest chair ever, but it has two female leads under the age of forty, which I think is pretty cool.

When Caroline asked me to speak this morning, I was very pleased to have the opportunity to explain why I decided to commit to being this year's Leadership Sponsor. There's two reasons.

The first is, at Gales we have a vision statement of "Fuelling Niagara for the next fifty years." We see it as our mission to do this in every way possible. Through petroleum products certainly, but also through our commitment to our corporate culture and through our philanthropic pursuits. As a regional company, we support, in some way, every municipality we service. Partnering with an organization like United Way, that serves every municipality in Niagara, was a no-brainer.

For the second reason, you need to know a bit more about me. I led a privileged childhood. I never had to worry if there was going to be food on my table, clothes on my back, or fuel in my furnace. However, that does not mean I took it for granted. Every day I watched my Dad go to work before the sun came up, and come home after the sun went down. I saw my parents volunteer in hundreds of different ways over the years. Special Olympics, Big Brothers/Big Sisters, Boys and Girls Club, Rotary — you name it and the Gale family, or *Gales Gas Bars*, has probably touched it.

Through volunteering, I saw first hand the other side of the spectrum. The individuals who weren't as lucky as me. The individuals who weren't sure when they would get their next meal, or if their clothes were warm enough, or didn't even have a home to put a furnace in. It made a huge impression on me.

At first, I was scared — being young and ignorant. Luckily, I quickly learned that those living in poverty, or suffering from mental or physical illness did not deserve my fear. They deserved my help. As I grew up, this grew into a curiosity into health care. I went to the University of Western Ontario, and achieved my Bachelor of Science in Nursing, and obtained a designation of Registered Nurse.

I returned home and practiced in the Niagara Health System, and the Niagara Region for five years. Then my life took a turn. I was a new mom to a little boy, and for the first six months I couldn't understand why when I looked at my little Eddie, I felt absolutely nothing. Not love, not hatred, not resentment, NOTHING. It was empty, it was strange, and it was scary. It was incredibly personal. No one knew what I was feeling — not even my husband. I made sure Eddie was fed, clothed, and bathed. However, other than when I was with my husband, I remained in my house because the thought of taking Eddie out, all by myself, was a task so huge that it caused crippling anxiety. I stayed inside, and handled him, and not much else. Not even making dinner, or doing the laundry.

I would call my husband at quitting time every day to make sure that he had left his office, and would not be late as I couldn't stand another moment by myself.

Slowly, life started turning around. Eventually, I was able

to recognize this for what it was — a six-month ordeal with significant postpartum depression. When I became pregnant again, this time with my daughter, I reached out to my closest circle and asked them to look for key indicators that meant it was happening again. This was the first they had heard of the struggles I'd had. I hid it very, very well.

It wasn't something I was willing to talk about. "Make sure I'm leaving the house," I said. Luckily this time there weren't any problems. However, knowing I didn't want to be cooped up in the house, my Dad approached me when my daughter was one-month old and asked if I'd like to be involved in a new project — the development of convenience stores within the company. Without knowing it, I made a pivotal decision at that moment. I embarked on a journey that would take me away from nursing entirely and throw me straight into the cut-throat world of business. I've been there ever since.

My point is, I've seen suffering, I've experienced suffering, and no one deserves to suffer.

When I joined Gales full-time, it gave me the ability to touch lives as more than a nurse at a bedside. I was able to find the time to volunteer again, eventually joining several boards and being a strong force behind organizations that help those that need it.

They say most startups fail within five years. They also say that most multi-generational businesses fail with the third generation. I'm very proud to say that I've now passed that five year mark, and we're doing extremely well.

So when Caroline called me and asked if I'd commit to being this year's Leadership Sponsor, I thought it was the right time to make a large commitment to an organization that resembles Gales. An organization that touches each municipality in Niagara.

At Gales, we're doing work internally to really invest in our employee culture, and I've taken time over the last year to stop and focus on my own personal growth. Both in my private and professional lives. I've thought a lot about what Gales means to me, what Niagara means to me, and what philanthropy means to me.

At the end of the day, one question sums it up. What do I want my legacy to be? One hundred years from now, how do I want to be remembered? The answer is simple — a good person. A person that others seek out for advice, for support, and for help. I want Niagara to benefit from having had me in it. I want my children to be proud that I was their mother.

My goal for Gales is to be an employer of choice. An employer that offers a fantastic work culture, and workplace environment — attracting and retaining superior employees. We've taken huge strides towards this over the last two years, with the most recent step being the commitment to being a Living Wage Champion.

At the beginning of my speech, I asked you for the first favour. Does everybody remember? In case you don't, the next time you see my Dad, you're going to say, "Are you Jessica's father?" Know that I'm doing a mental fist bump to you at that moment, and you'll probably get a chuckle out of my Dad.

So now for my second favour, I want you to think about what you want your legacy to be. One hundred years from now, what do you want Niagara to remember you for? I think you'll find that assisting United Way is only the first step.

Thank you.